DEALING WITH DIFFICULTY

A SYSTEMS APPROACH TO PROBLEM BEHAVIOUR

MARK PROVIS

Hodder & Stoughton
LONDON SYDNEY AUCKLAND

British Library Cataloguing in Publication Data

Provis, Mark
  Dealing with Difficulty: Systems Approach
  to Problem Behaviour
  I. Title
  371,93

  ISBN 0-340-56153-x

First published 1992

Typeset by Rowland Phototypesetting Limited, Bury St Edmunds, Suffolk
Printed in Great Britain for the educational publishing
division of Hodder & Stoughton Limited, Mill Road, Dunton Green,
Sevenoaks, Kent by St Edmundsbury Press Limited, Bury St Edmunds, Suffolk

Acknowledgments

This book represents experiences shared with a great many supportive colleagues.

My thanks to John Hardee who first gave me the space to work, to Peter Branston who provided the opportunity to design a systemic support service, to Mike de Val and Graham Bingham who showed sufficient trust for the service to thrive, and for the wider support provided by headteachers and their staff in mainstream schools. Thanks also to Pat Davies who always listened so thoughtfully.

My particular thanks to the staff of the support service especially my colleagues in the support team. This book really represents the experience of working with them but I alone am responsible for the viewpoints expressed.

I am especially grateful to Mary Payton – secretary, friend and support – without whom very little would ever have been finished.

Contents

No one is looking at the process. Everyone is too busy doing. There is a need for someone to do the thinking.

Sir John Harvey Jones
Start the Week, Radio 4
14.5.90

The social system writes the script for poor families.

Minuchin 1989

Introduction

This book brings together the experiences of fifteen years work with troubled children of one kind or another. The learning from such experiences was crystallised in the work of a team of education professionals who developed, practised and promoted an innovative approach to problem behaviour within educational settings.

The book aims to provide a framework for implementing approaches to problem behaviour to best effect. It is an opportunity to share with fellow professionals some working ideas that have proved to be very useful.

The first quote on the previous page underlines a central issue in the book – that to be effective in managing a troubled situation and to succeed in promoting positive change, requires the ability, skill and opportunity, to detach oneself from the immediacy of the problem and to examine it in process terms.

The key concepts explored in the book relate to the promotion of effective change. The ideas apply to looking in detail at how to manage a seemingly chronic behaviour problem in school/class/family, but work equally well in trying to effect change at the organisational level too. These ideas have been tried and tested in both primary and secondary settings. The text offers a candid account of the Team's activity and this means both enjoying its successes and sharing its mistakes.

The Team worked within one local education authority providing a complete system of support to schools regarding the management of difficult behaviour. It worked with ideas freely drawn from behavioural and psychodynamic psychology. With the case studies, readers may feel that they are covering familiar territory. The key difference in the Team's thinking was the use of these ideas within a *systemic* framework.

The title of the book has been carefully chosen – it is *not* about the maladjusted child; the troubled adolescent; the incompetent parent; the inexperienced member of staff; the 'stick in the mud' traditional teacher; or indeed any of those stereotypes that result in individuals being given *all* the blame for any particular problem. The book focuses upon the referred problem as being one that belongs *not* to the named individual but to everyone involved in the immediate subsystems operating around them. Indeed it goes one step further and suggests that the best solution lies with all concerned rather than with any component part. In other words, to achieve a positive change all must be engaged in its active promotion.

All the case study material has been drawn from direct practitioner activity, suitably amended (with fictional names) to protect the identity of the participants. The most recent material is drawn from the work of the team of support teachers who worked to understand and 'own' systemic thinking and apply it consistently in their interventions in schools.

Chapter 1

Where does systemic thinking fit?

There have been many overviews given of the range of interventions available to those who try to address the problem of difficult behaviour in schools. One of the most effective recent texts being that of Mongon et al. (1989). Such a detailed review will not be undertaken here – rather a summary is offered to show how 'systems thinking' provides a framework within which a range of approaches to problem behaviour can be used.

   The two principle modes of intervention with difficult behaviour come from different and at times polarised positions within the world of psychology. The following paragraphs highlight these differences with a summative description of each.

The psychodynamic approach

This assumes that the cause of problems lies somewhere in the recent or distant past and that the unearthing of such causes moves matters forward towards a solution. The discovery of these causes of problem behaviour may be achieved through counselling, play or enactment. Such an approach takes time; the worker needs to build the necessary rapport and trust for the process to work. This need for a combination of a great deal of time and private space being reserved in order to complete the given task has caused problems in the application of such an approach to school.

   Given the pressures upon our under-resourced schools there has been a reluctance to promote a method that uses so much professional time and one that does not have an obvious end point. Such approaches have tended to remain the province of the education social worker, the psychiatric day clinic and the residential school. The specialist skills available in such settings are not readily transferred into the ordinary classroom in schools.

Often the specialist settings have been slow to explain their approach to mainstream staff. Equally, many teachers within schools have been left wondering why their most overtly difficult and troubled pupils have not been deemed eligible for such intensive interventions, that is difficult adolescents in touch with the real world and aware of their behaviour may not be considered suitable for such an intervention. When such an approach has been attempted within schools, for example with the establishment of a school counsellor post, then other difficulties have emerged.

As the approach is time intensive, even though the post of counsellor may have been made full time, it has often proven difficult to time manage and to draw appropriate boundaries around referrals. Counsellors working one to one, or with small groups of pupils, have often found themselves overwhelmed with referrals. In trying to do too much, too quickly, using psychodynamic and humanistic approaches, the quality of their intervention and support has been jeopardised.

The school staff, under pressure themselves, often find it difficult, having just survived a challenging lesson, to accept that their more expert colleague had only been working with one pupil! Moreover, the psychodynamic approach works within a framework of extended confidentiality. There may be those who are outside the scope of the intervention, but continue to manage the day to day behaviour problems in class. They often struggle to discern progress being made and improvement effected.

Amongst some professionals working in this way there is a view that in helping a troubled adolescent face up to the cause of their difficulties, there may be a short-term deterioration as they start to try to confront the source of their problems.

In large schools, with large classes and a high pressure curriculum, teachers have often found it difficult to see that this type of intervention yields any benefit for them. Given the uncertain progress of such an intervention methodology, a major difficulty has been found trying to produce any clear evaluative evidence of its effectiveness.

A great deal of the evaluative evidence has been in the form of the case study narrative. Such detailed accounts of how problems can be solved seem both interesting and accessible. The difficulty for the busy professional in education has been to condense such reported practice into the small fragments of time available to them. There are very few occasions when school-based staff can sustain a commitment to this level of intervention with one pupil, over time.

For those interested in the full application of this approach, M. Rose (1990) writes about an intensive psychotherapeutic approach to troubled behaviour within one residential setting. The total commitment of a community to a particular style of work is both impressive and powerful.

The thinking and skills do not readily transfer to a school-based setting. Elements of the approach, for example the use of open questions to explore problems, may have begun to grow in schools but on the whole there is too little time to engage in such a sustained intervention.

The behaviourist approach

At the other extreme, the work of Skinner (1953) and Bandura (1973) has often entered the world of school in a highly mechanistic form. The model rests upon the concepts of:

stimulus ⟶ behaviour ⟶ reinforcement

that is there is an event or prompt – the stimulus. The individual makes a response to this – the behaviour. This response will be repeated depending upon the amount of reward – the reinforcement that the individual receives.

Behaviourist practitioners believe that given sufficient rigour, most behaviour is open to change through the effective management of both the stimulus and the reinforcement. The result is often a sustained change in behaviour rather than a transient one.

In education the model has become expressed as:

antecedents ⟶ behaviour ⟶ consequences

that is where the conditions that lead up to an action, can be the precipitating factor in initiating a behaviour. This behaviour will recur where the antecedents occur again or where the outcome from the behaviour in some way reinforces the individual in sustaining or repeating it.

This model can be used to help to comprehend why a problem behaviour starts and how it is sustained. A key issue in understanding the model is that the initial antecedents may have lapsed long ago. The prompt to the behaviour is less overt and less direct. In working with teacher colleagues it has often been difficult to identify the A→B→C linkage in clear unambiguous terms.

It is the concept of reinforcement that needs to be clearly grasped. It can have both negative and positive connotations. The key issue is its effect in sustaining or maintaining the particular behaviour.

Reinforcement can be in the form of good things such as adult attention, rewards (e.g. sweets), time at a favourite activity, or peer group attention etc. but may equally take the form of what teachers and parents may see as less good things, for example being sat apart from others, being sent from a classroom, or being sent to bed. All three of these may enable the individual to 'escape' from work or a difficult confrontation etc. The result is that whenever they wish to escape a situation, individuals may reach for the same learned response, that is the same provocative/annoying behaviour.

In managing the antecedents, to reduce the initial incidence of the behaviour and by direct manipulation of the reinforcing conditions, it is possible to make sustained changes in behaviour. One brief serious case study and one more lighthearted example may help to illustrate this approach.

Case study

Timothy, aged four, was referred by the headteacher of a large primary school for 'expert help'. The school was at the hub of a community that experienced many difficulties and was well used to managing its problems. Timothy was a little boy who seemed to simply ignore their usual sanctions and reward system and passed through the nursery class untouched and unaffected by the class teacher's concern.

In class Timothy did not make eye contact and did not speak directly to either adults or children. He would sidle up alongside some children and watch them play – particularly when they were using construction toys. At other times he would move alongside other children and bite them or pull their hair – seemingly without warning.

The classteacher felt quite rattled by Timothy as she was unable to discern any pattern to this activity; he did not have regular targets nor high status children who he shadowed at play. Using good parent-school links she explored the problem with the parents, but they seemed equally baffled yet did not share the teacher's concern about their son. They were proud of his phenomenal memory and quoted many examples of his ability to return to a situation and recall it in vivid detail.

The classteacher agreed that he was a potentially able boy and she too recalled instances when Timothy could find 'his' piece of paper amongst many – even when there seemed little to discriminate it from others. He had an eye for detail and seemed to be able to recognise instantly a detail that made a particular item or object unique.

The classteacher struggled on for some time, but a call for help was prompted by a television programme on gifted autistic children. She felt that Timothy showed many similar behavioural characteristics to those depicted by some of the children.

In behavioural terms it was very hard to spot the antecedents to Timothy's behaviour. Initially his behaviour seemed to be without pattern and almost random in its quality. Yet a sustained and detailed observation revealed that he always returned to particular activities and always began them again as if he had never left them. After much discussion with the classteacher it was agreed that what Timothy seemed to seek was non-involvement and non-contact with adults or children and that this was his reinforcement.

This idea was explored with his parents and it emerged that Timothy behaved in the same way at home. Furthermore, when he refused to do as they asked he was sent to his room. This was done coldly and unemotionally – both parents were anxious to explain that they did not shout. Timothy always responded by going upstairs. They explained that the kind of incident that prompted this behaviour could be anything from something as trivial as Timothy being asked to pick up an item he had dropped, to an issue as serious as an assault on his sister.

Further discussion revealed that Timothy's room was a positive treasure house with TV, video, computer and construction games. What is more, the room was a 'no go' zone to adults. If Timothy was in there, he only allowed them in by expressed permission.

In this instance this rather bizarre behaviour exhibited by Timothy is most effectively understood in terms of learned behaviour rather than in labelling it as a clinical condition.

The concepts of learned behaviour and behaviourism can be readily applied in schools *but* it seems to be important that we as education professionals accept that it does not just apply to children. If it explains pupil behaviour it can equally well be used to describe adult performance.

Antecedents	A heavy craft lesson is about to start. Alan does *not* enjoy heavy craft.
Behaviour	Alan enters the room and starts quarrelling with Diane and Paul about last week's project.
Consequence	The beginning of the lesson is delayed for twelve minutes.

Crucial to our understanding, insight and intervention is the fact that Alan teaches heavy craft.

Those interested in a readable account of such interventions might consult Bull and Sollity (1987), and for a clinic based approach Herbert (1975).

On first impression this model is simple and readily accessible. Psychologists have worked hard to promote this model of change as it has proven to be extremely time- and cost-effective. One outcome of this has been the 'Giving Behaviourism Away' movement, where psychologists have explained to teachers that they could take control of most difficulties by consistently applying these concepts, for example Wheldall and Merritt (1984).

Having given the psychology away there were certainly reported instances of teachers using the methodology with enthusiasm and securing success. However, some reservations have been expressed and psychologists working with teachers in schools have had to accept that on some occasions, with some problems, the behavioural technology has not been readily or effectively applied.

Seeming to be simple and easily accessible to all, the model has, at times, proven to be sophisticated, variable and has remained, in part, an expert practitioner's tool. In its simplest form this method can:

- be easily given away to teachers in school;
- be readily applied to solve what the writer would call linear problems;
- be used to develop a clear problem definition that is often found helpful in planning a focused intervention;

- lead to the design of readily monitored interventions;
- allow prompt refinement where necessary;
- produce a final result which should be evident to all concerned.

At times where the model has not been effective in schools it may be that the expectations have been unrealistic.

Or it may have been misapplied or misinterpreted.

Chapter 2

Bringing two views together

It is the author's view that behaviourist approaches provide an intervention tool which is both extremely powerful and effective. Its use brings a ready resolution to many problems. However, its danger is that complex problems can come to be viewed too simplistically. Complex entrenched problems are not best explained in linear terms. The author will argue that its application is most effective within the context of a wider understanding of individual behaviour coupled with the usage of significant interpersonal skills.

This view has evolved through practitioner experience and through committed application of the model and the ideas. The following case study may help to illustrate how psychodynamic work and the use of the behavioural model can be applied as complementary tools in effective interventions.

Case study

Amanda Williams was one of eight young people living in a family home for 'difficult to place' long stay children. The home was run on psychodynamic lines with staff working through the development of personal relationships with the children to help them come to terms with their disrupted past and to help them plan for positive futures. The core approach to their problems came through group discussion, individual exploration and counselling.

Amanda presented a severe challenge to all within the home – pushing children and staff to the limits of their self-control as she tried to confirm that she was both unloved and unlovable. A brief history highlights the complexity of her early experiences.

The Williams family had lived a volatile and violent life together, culminating in Mr Williams pushing Mrs Williams down the stairs. Mrs Williams, pregnant with her fourth child, miscarried. On hearing this news,

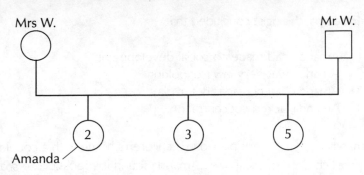

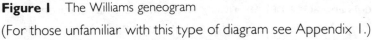

Figure 1   The Williams geneogram

(For those unfamiliar with this type of diagram see Appendix 1.)

Mr Brown, Mrs Williams' brother, went to the house and shot Mr Williams with a shotgun in front of the family. On her own for four to five months Mrs Williams functioned well, then the strain began to tell and she began to drink heavily whilst trying to rebuild her social life. Following Police and Social Agency involvement the Williams children were brought into care when all three children were found 'wandering at night (2.00 am), dressed in their underwear, in a filthy state, scrounging for food'.

There's no place like a home?

The two younger sisters were placed in care together. They moved home several times in four years as a 'more appropriate' group was sought for them. After four years they were fostered. The fostering broke down when the foster father left home. The sisters were immediately fostered again, this time with an authoritarian couple who hoped that the two little girls would cement their marriage. After some months the placement broke down as the girls were deemed to be 'incompatible with the foster parents' way of life'. Prior to leaving the home, the sisters learned that they were being replaced by an Afro-Caribbean baby. This knowledge left both sisters with feelings of racial ambivalence.

Reassessment

At the assessment centre Amanda called all female staff 'Mummy'. She was restless, unable to sleep and ran away from all male staff. She screamed, spat, kicked and yelled abuse – often directed towards herself. At other times she sat and wailed, tearlessly for an hour or more.

The centre's psychologist concluded that:

1. Amanda had made no social development.
2. Amanda was very inward looking.
3. Amanda had no capacity for play.
4. Amanda lacked concentration.

Next, Amanda and Jane were placed in a children's home with a couple who had two small children of their own. Amanda found it impossible to share the houseparents and acted out her rivalry with the two small children. Unable to manage Amanda's behaviour the staff allowed her to hide under the table or to lock herself inside a shed. The placement lasted for two-and-a-half years. In that time Amanda was placed in a special class and deemed 'unreachable and unteachable'. One Easter the houseparents left the home suddenly, without notice. It emerged later that Amanda felt she had been the person who had driven them out with her 'power'.

There followed three sets of temporary houseparents who on average lasted one month in post. New permanent staff were finally appointed who reported, 'Amanda is a pretty child but with her hair worn like a curtain to her chin. Her shoulders are very hunched and she curves forward with a pronounced stoop. Her movements are very awkward and clumsy.'

Having established that there was no organic cause to her difficulties, further expert guidance was sought. The advice given was:

–   to encourage Amanda to explore her environment;
–   to encourage the other children to tolerate her acting out behaviour;
–   to give Amanda guidance on appearance and self-presentation;
–   to absorb the pressure Amanda would generate as she tested everyone's commitment;
–   to engage Amanda in an exploration of her history.

Gradually Amanda began to develop fantasy games using toy horses and Afghan hounds. The theme was a constant one:

–   the horse/dog in danger;
–   the horse/dog being rescued by a girl;
–   the farmer/owner giving the girl the animal.

This drama was repeated in many different contexts but was always a solo performance. Amanda could not tolerate another child/adult joining in.

At this time Amanda's verbal interactions with adults and children were very clipped and abrupt: 'Money?' meant 'Can I have my pocket money.' Amanda continued to act out, two or three times a day. These incidents were extreme, with Amanda hurling herself at doors and walls, beating at herself and others whilst screaming at full volume. One often repeated phrase was 'When I get my husband I will kill you'. At times such whirlwind sessions could last over two hours.

Further help was sought. A psychiatrist described Amanda as a 'borderline psychotic' child with no clear notion of self. He recommended staff continue to absorb Amanda's violence and anger and that they care for and reach out to her during her acting out episodes. He felt that the prognosis was poor and that Amanda would always require some form of institutional placement to survive.

There followed two years of relative stability. At one point Amanda broke the neck of her pet rabbit for scratching her. Her response was fascinating – she was shocked that the rabbit did not recover. This seemed to release a flood of memories about her early familial experiences. Amanda then continued to speak about these memories from time to time – often as if they were events that happened to someone else.

After two years, staff in a review discussion, suggested that there was a perceptible qualitative shift in Amanda's acting out behaviour. Several people agreed that this acting out behaviour was much more under Amanda's control and direction than in the past. There was a suggestion that Amanda's need to vent her inner chaos had lessened. There followed an intense and earnest discussion as to whether changing the staff's response to Amanda's acting out behaviour might not cause the symptom of her distress to disappear but leave the underlying cause untouched. Some felt that her fragile damaged ego needed to continue to discharge the pent up emotional energy resulting from her early experiences.

The decision to change the caring approach was determined by the fact that Amanda had less than three years left in local authority care. This decision was validated when it was discussed with Amanda. She differentiated between 'having a mood' – her acting out behaviour – to 'getting angry at being criticised' – the new quality that the staff were describing. Furthermore, showing far greater insight than any of the team had suspected, she said 'Once I get angry, I just don't know how to stop.'

The behaviour programme

Given Amanda's own description of what was happening to her the key task seemed to be to separate out her 'emotional collapse and loss of self-control' from her 'intentional aggression to avoid situations which she found unpleasant'.

Establishing the baseline

There were violent outbursts on six days out of seven during the first week of monitoring Amanda's behaviour. These were not equivalent events, they varied from a localised explosion to some two to three hours of raging. The staff team examined the antecedents – the events leading up to Amanda's outbursts – but could not discern any particular pattern or events that were under their control.

The team agreed to monitor Amanda's behaviour for a second week and that some time after each incident the member of staff concerned would approach her and discuss the situation and how it had arisen. Amanda offered one of two responses to this – total self-forgetting, that is no memory of the incident, or saying 'It's all your fault'.

In the former instance she blankly denied that an incident of any substance had taken place. In the second case she would blame the member of staff and the discussion would rapidly escalate towards renewed confrontation. Faced with this behaviour it proved very difficult to negotiate any procedure or contract with Amanda.

The team finally agreed that four out of six incidents were examples of Amanda's intentional aggression. This attempt at objectivity was grounded in pooling their subjective views of whether an incident was intentional aggression or simply her 'loss of control'. This data formed the initial baseline from which Amanda's subsequent progress was measured.

Phase 1

Drawing upon the work of Herbert (1975) where behavioural control seemed to be presented within a caring framework, the programme began as follows:

MON	TUES	WED	THURS	FRI	SAT	SUN
✱	✱		✱		✱	✱

Figure 2 Amanda's behavioural chart

A behavioural chart was pinned to a cork noticeboard in the kitchen (see Figure 2 above). On the chart Amanda gained one star for each day that there was no acting out behaviour. The accumulation of nine stars would entitle Amanda to a horseriding lesson at a local stable. The lesson was always booked two weeks in advance in Amanda's presence. A riding lesson was used as the ultimate positive reinforcement as horses had always loomed large in Amanda's interests. (The interval of two weeks was simply a matter of budgetary constraint!)

The obvious weakness of the programme was that once Amanda had transgressed on any one day she was unable to redeem herself and secure a star for that day. However, she did not seem to take advantage of this situation and escalate her temper when a star was lost.

Throughout the course of the programme Amanda received a lot of encouragement and positive reinforcement from the other members of the group. Initially she was highly motivated and secured the first two riding lessons with stars to spare – a clear indication that with sufficient reward or reinforcement she could exercise greater self-management and control over a whole four-week period. It was agreed that there would be no carry over of stars from one fortnightly period to the next.

The third fortnightly sequence proved to be traumatic. Amanda experienced new pressure in school due to a change of class and at home lost her sister every Saturday as she had obtained casual work. Amanda could not manage these changes and the result was that she lost the third riding lesson. Staff spent significant time discussing these difficulties with Amanda who came up with the following description as to what happened to her during her outbursts: 'Going stiff and red inside my head'.

Phase 2

This description of Amanda's behaviour prompted the staff to try to provide additional support and strategies to help her cope. Being focused upon outcome, rather than committed to a one-theory based system of working, they drew upon the concepts of *(a)* relaxation techniques and *(b)* cognitive behavioural rehearsal.

(a) Relaxation techniques
[Drawn from Rimm et al. (1971) and then O'Donnell and Warnell (1973).] This approach is based upon the idea that deep muscle relaxation and aggression are incompatible physical states. In teaching subjects to be able to relax themselves there is an expectation that they will then have a physical mechanism to control their rage.

Amanda practised this approach for twenty minutes each day after school. She began to enjoy it and on difficult days in school would rush home to relax herself! It is impossible to separate out the key factor in this – the adult attention, the development of a personal skill, or the discovery of the relaxed state.

(b) Cognitive behavioural rehearsal
Drawing upon the work of Miechenbaum (1972) the team tried to augment Amanda's changed behaviour by working to enable her to change her cognitive viewpoint. The steps in such an approach are shown below:

Steps	Amanda's script
1. Specify the problem.	'I must stay calm.'
2. State the demands needed to cope with this problem.	'The problem will only last a minute.'
3. Use a series of self-instructions to perform the required task.	'I will sit down with my arms by my sides and relax.'

4. Use imagery to devise a solution.	'I can stay calm like Watso' (imagery using a revered figure – in this case her favourite horse).
5. Having dealt with the problem make self-rewarding statements.	'I knew I could do it if I wanted to.'

This script was rehearsed many times with Amanda. During rehearsals Amanda's performances had to be carefully shaped. (There was some suggestion that the self-statements should be even shorter as she could escalate so fast. On balance it was felt that the script helped her to maintain her concentration on task.)

The most difficult phase was when Amanda was encouraged to move from audible verbal self-statements to the point where they were quietly whispered. It was some time before she internalised the process and managed it in silence.

The next four weeks of the programme worked well. Amanda's emotional collapses were much less frequent, though there was some suggestion that they were, if anything, more severe when they did occur. Over the next two months the programme became steadily more demanding as the reward system was changed, but Amanda coped well. So much so that her teacher in school made the point that on two separate occasions she had been surprised to see Amanda actively control her outburst and switch it off.

All problems over?

Four months on, and over lunch it emerged that the rest of the children in the group felt that Amanda's problem behaviour was now solved and that there was a need to stop rewarding her for behaviour that was part of every day normal expectation for the rest of the group. It was in fact Amanda who solved this problem. She followed her sister's example and got a job lasting two hours on a Friday and Saturday, cleaning up in a local hairdressers. The money from this job paid for riding lessons. To everyone's surprise it became evident that in a six month period Amanda had changed to become a candidate for a semi-independence programme.

Having succeeded in supporting Amanda through a sustained period of effective change, reflecting upon the experience resulted in some tentative conclusions.

1. Deeply entrenched problems were not readily solvable.

2. In such situations solutions had to be 'lived' twenty-four hours per day to be effective.

3. The psychodynamic approach helped in *understanding* and *gaining insight* into Amanda's difficulties.

4. This, in turn, enabled the team to manage her behaviour with firmness and empathy.

5. The sense of completeness of our insight, coupled with the evident warmth in our daily contact with her enabled us to consider the use of a behavioural programme.

6. In a domestic regime where much of her environment could come under direct adult control the behavioural programme represented a significant powerful rewarding system.

7. The programme brought effective discernable results.

8. It did not and could not provide a cure all.

As a professional practitioner who moved from residential social work to day educational settings, one began to feel that there were many problems that were inaccessible to behavioural interventions in school, largely because the children's external environment was often too chaotic and unpredictable for the reward levels to ever be sufficiently consistent and powerful.

The discovery of systems theory and systemic interventions seemed to provide a fresh approach to overcoming the problems of inconsistency and fragmentation when planning interventions, providing an epistemology or way of thinking that enabled behavioural and psychodynamic approaches to be effectively integrated.

Chapter 3

Systems theory

A different way of thinking

General systems theory was a new paradigm developed by Van Bertalanffy in the 1940s. It made a profound impact upon the physical sciences and from the mid 1960s onwards started to influence thinking in the social sciences. The author's first encounter with this way of thinking was as a geography A level student studying hydrology – the water cycle.

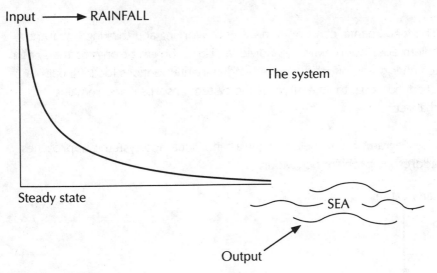

Figure 3   The water cycle

The thinking suggests that:

— *input*, in this case rainfall,
— moves as *energy* through the system
— leaving as *output*.

The shape of the system is in a state of *dynamic equilibrium*, that is it changes in response to increased input and to changed output but will then return to its original shape or 'steady state'. In other words, the system was quite resilient and able to absorb a great deal of energy without much change.

To transform the system into a new and different shape required a huge amount of energy or a dramatic event. Under such circumstances change takes place and is evident throughout the system and not just at one point of it – the whole system will in some way be altered. The one concept being that change is the result of change throughout the system and not in any individual or compartmentalised part of it.

At the time the author found these ideas both holistic and satisfying and found that geography was much more interesting as a result. It was some years later when reading Bateson's work with troubled families (1972) that the potential of systemic thinking for enabling change in schools became apparent. It was Minuchin's work (1974) that provided the schema to turn this potential into practice. There is now a huge body of knowledge and experience of using this approach when trying to work with family systems. The most populist text is Skynner and Cleese's book *Families and How to Survive Them* (1983).

The fundamental concept in this way of working and thinking is that the problem does not lie with the individual. The problem belongs to the system. Much energy and effort can be expended in interventions focusing upon a labelled individual to little effect as the system absorbs it and remains unchanged.

The diagrams below help to contrast individual and systemic approaches to addressing problem behaviour.

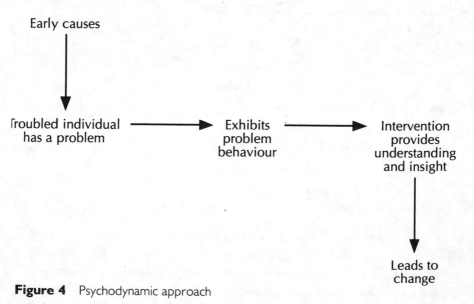

Figure 4 Psychodynamic approach

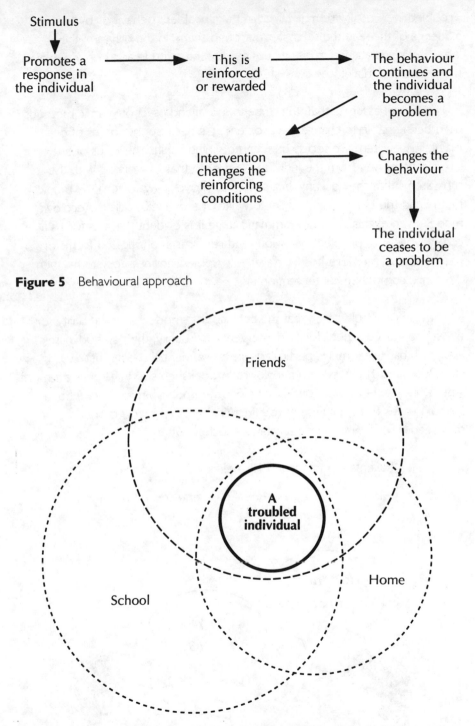

Figure 5 Behavioural approach

Figure 6 Systemic methods. (The diagram shows that the individual operates within a series of overlapping systems. The people in these systems interact with the individual and with each other.)

Troubled individuals are maintained in their problem behaviour by the influence of those in the subsystems around them. In the diagram, the individual is maintained in his/her position by the attitude and behaviour of those involved in all three subsystems.

The model assumes that where behavioural and psychodynamic methods have been unable to change the problem, it is because the forces of one maintaining system are too strong. This definition shifts the focus of the intervention away from the individual and onto that of working with the subsystems that they occupy. In a sense the move is away from the medical model and the behavioural model to what Upton (1990) calls the ecological model. Even at this initial diagrammatic stage it is evident that this forms a complex view of problem behaviour and requires sophisticated forms of intervention. The more hostile, negative or polarised the subsystems, then the more complex the intervention task.

The author would argue that the behaviourist model has great utility for the school-based school-focused intervention. Equally, the psychodynamic approach has great merit, particularly in the residential therapeutic setting (see Rose, 1990). The systemic/ecological model seems to have greatest merit where the teacher/educational psychologist-led behavioural intervention in school proves to be insufficient to effect change. Experienced practitioners may readily recognise the circumstances such as when:

1. Parents cannot 'hear' that their child is a problem.

2. Participants in a problem take up entrenched positions.

3. The adults themselves fall into a mutual blaming relationship and the problem remains.

It is at this point that systemic thinking can be effectively used to provide a way forward.

Open and closed systems

Traditional approaches to addressing problem behaviours tend to approach matters as if they occur within a closed system.

Closed systems

If we take a particular problem, such as the use of bad language by a pupil in a lesson, schools often respond by focusing more and more resources upon that problem behaviour.

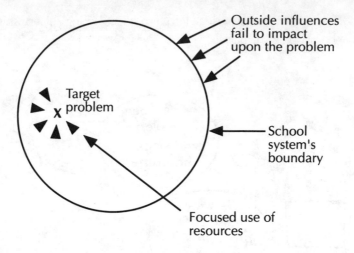

Figure 7 A closed system

Such resources might be the classroom teacher's time and attention. If that fails – the involvement of a colleague or more senior member of staff. If that fails the use of a deputy headteacher and, ultimately, the headteacher. This escalation continues, adding more and more resources until the problem is resolved or the pupil excluded. The unforeseen effect of this escalation is the confirmation to the pupil that they are in fact a bigger or more important problem than they first thought.

At some point there may be an attempt to involve the pupil's parents in dealing with the matter. However, staff in schools have very little intensive training in how to optimise the outcome from such encounters. Teachers can inadvertently blame the parents, may be unaware that the parent's own school experiences were unhappy ones and most importantly may misread silence or acquiescence as confirmation of the parents' willingness to support the school. Ways of approaching such meetings are explored later on in this book. (The best starting point to involving parents in the resolution of a difficulty is to have a history of positive dialogue to call upon. Interventions are much more difficult when there is no history of contact or where the scale of the problem comes as a surprise to the parents.)

The above approach assumes that there is a problem that can be solved and that the practitioners have sufficient control to ensure a solution. Such a view is often disproved in practice, with the problem behaviour persisting or worsening and ultimately the school subsystem gets transformed through the use of exclusion or truancy.

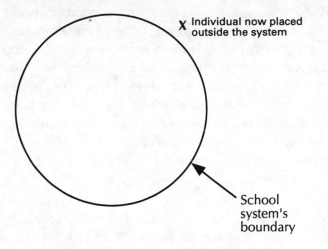

Figure 8 Exclusion – a system's failure

As mature professionals within education there is a need to see this as a system's failure. We as adults and knowledge bearers have failed to enable a pupil to change or grow. It may be that the failure is inevitable but there is a need to ensure that the school has eliminated all possible ways of effecting change first.

One key yet rarely used approach is to see the need to approach interventions as if they take place within 'open' systems.

Open systems

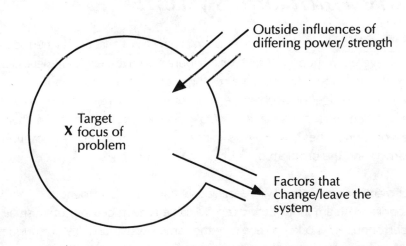

Figure 9 An open system

The worker in an open system realises that the throughput/input of external factors may far outweigh the impact of his/her immediate resources. Severe difficulties at home may well prevent a pupil being able to respond to a behavioural intervention in school. Given this awareness the worker, whether teacher, psychologist or social worker, does not focus all his/her resources upon the problem. The problem is redefined as being a product of the system. The worker therefore tries to use the resources within the system together with appropriate use of the outside influences to work for change. It is important to note that the effort is *not to solve or end the problem but to make progress.*

Such an attitude recognises that once any kind of change is under way it is very difficult to predict or control the direction it will take. Indeed, it is for those who are participating in this change to determine the outcome. Successful and sustained change is the sort that the participants define and decide for themselves. Many difficulties are resolved by schools and families because they are able to absorb and accommodate change. The need for additional help or intervention only comes when the system has rigidified and cannot respond appropriately.

This text is concerned with reporting attempts to make effective interventions in open systems using a range of techniques to promote positive change.

More than one system

Since the referred problem is generally in the form of a label attached to the child: an aggressive pupil; a truant; or a hyperactive five-year-old, there is a danger that the label influences the response of the teachers who immediately manage the problem. A head of year may receive a referral for aggressive behaviour in class and begin by confronting the pupil for his/her aggression. Sometimes this proves sufficient – the pupil accepts the caution or warning and the problem diminishes.

Yet many heads of year will recognise the fact that they spend a disproportionate amount of their very valuable time in dealing with a small number of pupils who keep repeating the same behaviour – 'return business'. Indeed, in some instances, the whole process gets viewed with some cynicism with both pupils and teachers seeing the interview/confrontation as

Mr/Ms 'doing their act'. In systems terms such a process is labelled 'more of the same'. In other words, the energy spent in trying to deal with a problem is used in a repeat performance of a form of intervention that has already failed. The very fact that the same pupil is back again suggests that something is not working.

In systems terms what was intended as being a form of intervention for change has become part of the problem. Perhaps an example adapted from Upton and Cooper (1990) might illustrate this process:

– David sees his teacher as picking on him.
– The teacher expects David to misbehave.
– David wanders off-task in class.
– His teacher anticipates a developing problem and redirects him to task.
– David sees other pupils off-task who are not spoken to.
– David stares at another's child's 'off-task' behaviour.
– The teacher feels David is ignoring him and redirects David to task.
– David explodes at this 'injustice'.
– The teacher sends for the deputy headteacher who removes David from the lesson.
– David's parents are summoned to school and told of the incident.
– David returns home that night to an explosive row from his parents.
– David tries to fight back, then breaks down and cries telling his parents of the 'teacher picking on him'.
– His parents feel guilty about their initial anger with David and try to encourage him to manage the teacher in a different way.
– David returns to class convinced the teacher picks on him, and armed with an impression that home will support him.
– The teacher enters the class and looks to see how David managed the telling off from his parents.

BANG

This process has been described as 'circularity'. Each of the two participants is contributing to an ongoing cycle of behaviour. Systems practitioners would accept the same referral but view it in a different way. They would try to restate the problems, seeing them as not being solely the produce of internal processes operating within the pupil. Rather they would be seen as resulting from the constantly changing sequences of interactions around him/her.

This is a much more complex view of referrals but one which the author argues is much more related to the reality that the pupils experience. It may be very difficult for teachers having attempted to solve a problem by what might be called 'linear methods', to accept that their aim, communication and practice should shift to seeing the problem as a product of the sequences of interactions and that their task will be to intervene to effect change in a positive direction. In diagrammatic terms the difference becomes more apparent as shown in Figure 10.

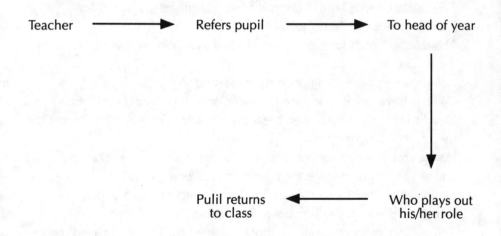

Figure 10   The linear model

Clearly where this type of referral is getting repeated then the head of year is expending precious pastoral time in what starts to appear to be redundant activity. The author argues that to break into this cycle the head of year, or the next person in the referral hierarchy, would need to restate the problem and therefore the solution, in systems terms – see Figure 11. The referer then needs to explore where the problem is at its worst and where there is no problem at all. Such an exploration defines the limits of the problem and at the same time raises areas wherein may lie the resources to develop a sustaining solution.

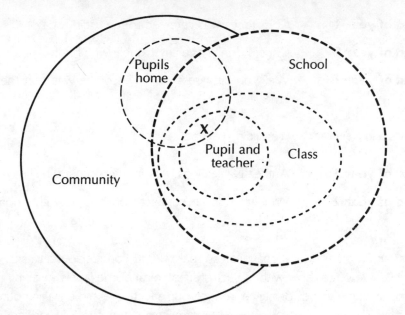

Figure 11 Examining the systems of which a pupil is a part

It may be that within the wider system an intervention would need to focus upon working with a number of *subsystems* such as: parent and child; teacher and pupil; teacher and parents; teacher, parents and child; teacher, grandparents, parent and child; teacher and teacher colleagues . . . and so on. This is not to suggest that *all* subsystems have to be worked with on *every* occasion. It becomes a matter of practised skilled judgement as to which offer the greatest potential for success given existing time constraints. However, there is a risk of working too narrowly too quickly, as the practitioner is redefining the problem in terms of the subsystems that they engage with.

At first glance pastoral staff may consider this form of analysis as being too detailed and too difficult given the demands made upon them. The author's argument is that for those pastoral staff who find that they are over-committed to the management of a handful of pupils and failing to engage with the vast majority of pupils for whom they are responsible, this approach may, with practice, prove more cost effective in time terms.

There are difficulties in pursuing such an approach, as is clear from both Figure 11 and the list of subsystems that such an analysis may imply 'blame' being attributed to colleagues and/or parents as well as to the child. Indirectly this happens at times in school, for example:

Head of year 1	Chris Jones was referred to me *again* today!
Head of year 2	Chris? I don't have any trouble with him!
Head of year 1	Well you can guess whose lesson he was in at the time.

and again in a similar way regarding parents . . .

| **Head of year 1** | Anthea Davies was back in my room again today. |
| **Head of year 2** | Well what do you expect from the kid with a home like that. |

Whilst we might as educational professionals, like to consider ourselves as objective, we often carry with us such stereotypical blame labels. In doing so we impair our own performance, reduce our effectiveness in engaging others in positive change and contribute to our own stress (the issue of working without blame will be explored later on).

In developing an appropriate use of systemic thinking professionals need to work with a positive attitude in even entrenched situations. Such a positive approach ensures that others feel able and empowered to effect change.

Systemic thinking and education

There have been attempts to develop systemic approaches to issues in education in the UK. These have tended to be in the form of whole-school approaches to problems, as discussed by Burden (1978) for example. In attempting to work this way Burden was training educational psychologists on the Exeter University course. There is a strong case for developing such thinking from an early stage but the use of this kind of approach by established senior teachers in a small project team would, in all likelihood, lead to further and wider systemic change as the deliverers would have greater credibility in school. Nonetheless, as Upton and Cooper (1990) point out, there is now an established body of knowledge, skills and techniques for addressing problems in families and this has been extended to problems in organisations but there has been little evidence of this approach being extended to working with behavioural difficulties within UK educational settings.

Authors have drawn attention to the potential of such a way of working, for example Shuttleworth (1982) and Speed (1984). From a clinic based setting Dowling and Osborne (1985) have tried to describe a number of examples of good practice that have attempted to bridge the gap between the clinic and the school. Nevertheless, these ideas do not seem to have been taken up and developed within the UK and there is little evidence of its usage in educational literature.

Upton and Cooper (*ibid*) speculate as to why this is the case and offer some tentative possibilities:

- *The relevance [of systemic thinking] is not immediately apparent.*

- *They [systemic ideas] challenge too many of our assumptions about the nature of emotional and behavioural problems in schools.*

- *They have been rejected as too threatening.*

The writer will argue that the real problem is somewhat different:

- That the concept of systemic thinking proves to be initially attractive to many.
- The subconcepts that make up the approach are less tangible and therefore less easy to acquire.
- Even having acquired such concepts it is difficult to articulate them to others.
- The skills required to utilise these concepts are most readily learned within a group who transact in a common systemic language and apply this within their work.
- The group needs to constantly work to refine its skills and its conceptual thinking in order to sustain its effective performance.

Having briefly reviewed the overall concept of systemic thinking, the remainder of this book will attempt to address these problems in turn by:

- Describing the subconcepts that make up one particular version of the model.
- Examining the skills that are needed to develop and implement this way of working in education.
- Exploring the application of these skills through some examples of detailed casework and through some interactive self-assessment materials.

- Sharing the process used in developing one team's thinking – both the potential and the pitfalls of working in this way.

Finally, the book will explore the wider issue of how such practice might fit within the overall system within a local education authority and refer to particular experience of this.

The systems model

Having had the experience of using systemic thinking and applying it practically within a clinical context, the author was anxious to try to utilise the power of these ideas within his own professional context – education. This required a scrutiny of the many models and ideas that have been generated within the new paradigm.

In the event, the author utilised the concepts developed by Minuchin (1974) that have been described within the overall terminology of systems thinking as a 'structuralist' approach. As will become clear, such ideas readily lend themselves to usage in schools whereas some of the strategic–systemic school ideas (Palazzoli et al., 1989) might be deemed too esoteric and in other ways inappropriate for an educational milieu.

The account that follows is therefore not a coherent overview of the whole of systems thinking – for that readers might turn to Speed (1984) – rather it is the integration of some of these concepts into a working body of ideas that could be applied within schools. In the application of some of these ideas they may be stretched beyond their progenitor's original intention as they are adapted to a school context.

Key concepts

There are a number of key concepts that underpin one's thinking in planning systems interventions. These need to be understood at the outset and incorporated into the practitioner's attitudinal stance. They may not necessarily be explicitly referred to in their day to day practice.

1. Homeostasis

This very technical term can be readily understood as the state of dynamic equilibrium. This means that even where open systems are subject to the effects of input and disturbance from outside they will tend to maintain a position of dynamic stability. At a given point in time this might be described as a 'steady state' but this term does not truly convey the system's ability to absorb energy and effort. Colleagues who have tried to implement radical change within a school system may, at times, have worked with huge energy and commitment only to see this result in notional change, with the system seemingly able to absorb the more radical elements of their reforms. In effect this is to experience the systems process of homeostasis at work.

Even where individuals have a proven track record of being effective in another school/department and have been brought in to promote a similar change, it is often the case that in the new context their efforts are neutralised, their energy absorbed and the changes that they effect are little more than cosmetic ones. Once this central idea is understood it becomes clear that extra effort and energy on behalf of one person is unlikely to procure an effective shift or change. The caricature of multi-memo writers perhaps illustrates this well. They expend high energy writing to secure *what should be*, without working with everyone to enable them to *move from what is to what might be*.

Having understood this concept of homeostasis the next step is to digest the key implication, which is that: individuals are unlikely to make impact if they work alone. They cannot make sufficient impact on the system by themselves. To change a system it is necessary to involve as many people as possible in promoting that change.

Securing this involvement requires specific skills and a particular way of working. Involving many people may mean securing a degree or level of change that is not quite or not all of the change that was required. Inevitably it means accepting that the ideal/perfect change is unlikely. In involving many other people it becomes difficult to control the pace of the change and its direction. However, the act of involvement, particularly if it focuses upon *empowering* the individuals concerned, is more likely to lead to effective and self-sustaining change.

Referring back to the example of David (p. 33) it is possible to see that the teacher–pupil system is maintained by:

1. The teacher construing David as a 'very aggressive boy' and interacting with him in these terms.
2. David categorising the teacher as 'always picking on me'.

This relationship is maintained in the form of a guarded hostility. As more energy is applied to solve the problem the system adjusts with a more energised response on the other side. In adding more and more power to his position, the teacher is inadvertently raising the level of readjustment that will follow.

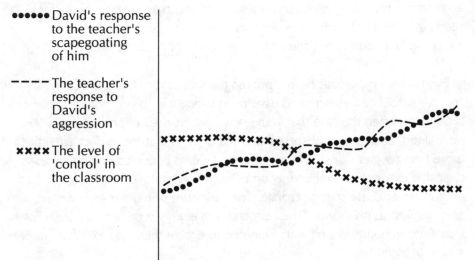

●●●●● David's response to the teacher's scapegoating of him

− − − − The teacher's response to David's aggression

✗✗✗✗ The level of 'control' in the classroom

Figure 12   The changing balance in the interaction between David and the classteacher

In trying to address this problem solely through the use of a linear intervention programme more and more energy becomes focused upon the interaction between David and Mr Jones, the teacher.

Mr Jones responds to David's aggression with what he sees as appropriate concern.

David experiences this concern as hostility and responds accordingly.

Mr Jones sees David's response as rejecting his proper concern and further confirmation of David's aggression and so designs a programme to reinforce David's appropriate non-aggressive behaviour.

David rejects the low-level rewards that a school can offer a teenager.

Mr Jones is reinforced in his view that this particular boy is unchanging and unchangeable as, after all, not even he Mr Jones has managed to make a difference.

This type of entrenched interaction is quite common in ongoing problem situations. Mr Jones has applied his professional skill to develop a linear solution that results in the pupil feeling even more rejected by the school as represented by Mr Jones. Equally, Mr Jones, who has tried to use the advice he gathered at an in-service course, or from an educational psychologist, is left feeling that the intervention programme has been a lot of fuss to little purpose, and abandons it.

In terms of the professional development of the educationist the saddest aspect of the situation is that Mr Jones has proven to be open to ideas, flexible and committed to try on behalf of the pupil. It is often the motivated staff who can become disenchanted as the less motivated will not have given their initial commitment to such a programme at the outset!

In systems terms Mr Jones and David have assumed positions of *complementarity*. The behaviour of one is inadvertently contributing to the maintenance of the behaviour of the other. This forms a key feature in many entrenched problem referrals. The very behaviour that is being referred is

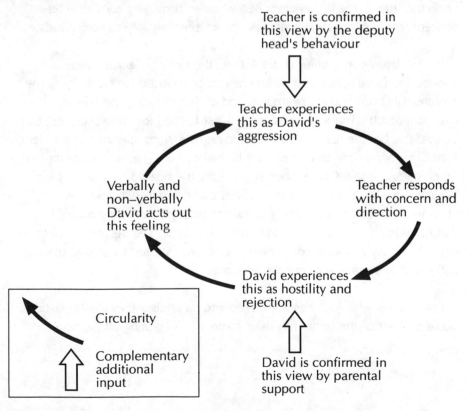

Figure 13   Reinforcing the complementary cycle

dependent upon the behaviour of and interaction with the other elements of the system. Even when a solution was sought beyond the immediate participants, through the deputy head and the parents, no progress was made. All concerned behaved with the best of intentions to no good effect.

In this instance we have examined a brief snapshot in time, where the ultimate end may be the fragmentation of the system. In systems terms this is a change but only in response to crisis, that is the complete abandonment of the old system. However, it is not unimaginable that where heads of year move up through the school with their year groups, such a relationship, begun in year one, may be maintained throughout the pupil's secondary school career. A useful analogy might be to see the pupil and the teacher locked into a dance. The rhythm may change, the tempo may get faster, the movement at times more violent, nevertheless the pair rely upon each other to sustain the performance! On one occasion in sharing this insight with a senior pastoral colleague he turned and said 'Well I never thought of myself as a dancing master.' It felt like a rejection of a tentative insight offered to someone with whom I had built a relationship of significant trust. Reflecting upon this later in the day I questioned whether conveying such abstract concepts through concrete analogies was an effective way to communicate.

Weeks later, over coffee at break time, the same colleague in speaking about a fourth year boy with whom he had been locked in battle for some months, said 'You know Christopher and all that shouting and bawling – well I just stopped the music.' Somewhat at a loss I asked for an explanation, to be told that he, the teacher, had realised his role in maintaining the problem with Christopher. He described how he had come to realise that all the other staff now saw Christopher as being his, the head of year's, problem. What's more he, as head of year, noticed that not only was he expending huge amounts of energy in giving Christopher lengthy dressing downs but that this was having no impact on Christopher at all. The outcome was that he had radically reappraised his own strategy and started to engage the wider staff in a more appropriate response.

For readers who feel they are locked into an endless dance with particular pupils the rest of the book may offer some way of getting off the floor.

Interactional patterns

Behavioural psychologists have worked hard within education to try to encourage teacher colleagues to describe a referred pupil's behaviour in objective terms. The kind of referral that causes concern might be one couched in such language as, 'Mary is *always* late for class, she *never* does any work and shows *no* interest in taking part in class discussions.'

The compiler of a report that includes such a paragraph may well conclude that they have done a good job. They have described aspects of Mary's behaviour in class, indeed in these three lines have stated an opinion about her timekeeping, work production and attitude. A behavioural psychologist or a senior pastoral teacher may respond to such a referral by asking for objective data, rather than the use of such absolute phrases.

In this particular example they may ask for:

—   An attendance diary – time of arrival in lesson.
—   A work record for a given week.
—   A sample of classroom behaviour obtained through a systematic observation exercise.

Such information is used to provide a baseline for current performance so that once a programme is implemented, early success can be measured and positively reinforced to promote change. Such striving for objectivity is laudable and the more accurate reportage has resulted in enhanced school-based interventions. Early effort by the pupil can readily be recognised by the classteacher who, through the programme, has a legitimate means of rewarding the pupil's effort without necessarily obtaining perfect behaviour.

The pursuit of clarity of language and objective understanding should be supported by all. However, to review this particular referral the subjective language may also prove helpful. 'Mary is *always* late for class, she *never* does any work and shows *no* interest in taking part in class discussions.' The italic typeface highlights the teacher's use of absolutes in the referral of the pupil and perhaps is indicative of the level of her exasperation. It may be that a teacher in such a position will find it hard to strive for objectivity even after attempting to draw a baseline.

The author would argue that to ensure the success of the behavioural/linear intervention programme there is a need for objective measurement and understanding. However, some problems, due to the systems response, are not resolved in this way. When colleagues encounter such a situation there is a need to intervene in a different way rather than do 'more of the same'. In working with referred problems within a systems framework the author found it most useful to accept that the referring staff found it difficult to hold on to an objective detached position with the pupil. In fact it was the subjective information – the levels of anger, annoyance and frustration – that provided the most helpful clues to an effective way forward. If the 'problem' is not construed as the referred pupil but is to be *reframed* as the interaction(s) between the pupil and the member(s) of staff, then third party objective data is unlikely to be readily available.

Beginning from a systems position, the worker is anxious to hear from both teacher(s) and pupil their subjective views of events and their feelings about a given situation. In other words systems practitioners are concerned with understanding the interactions, attitudes and perceptions that operate around a referred problem. This becomes very clear at secondary level where a referred pupil may experience very dysfunctional interactions with two or three members of staff, yet very successful interactions with others. The systems interventionist works with this information to strive for a positive solution.

A further element to understanding such interventional patterns may be to view them in terms of appropriate stage development. Some family systems practitioners characterise families as evolving in their function:

A forming stage Where two adults marry/live together and strive to reconcile the demands of their 'old systems'. A time when each partner will give up some of their old ways of living but struggle to retain elements that were important or successful to them.

A parenting stage Where the pair now struggles to adjust to the demands of a third member of the group.

A mature stage Where the pair copes with the struggle of living with the demands and pressures of supporting an emerging adult.

An old age stage Where the pair is a couple again and they work to fill the space left by the departed children. Problems at this stage are sometimes called the 'empty nest syndrome'.

There is much adaptation and accommodation required of the participants as the family moves through these stages.

1. Adaptation to new circumstances, for example, having a home together.
2. Accommodation – creating time, space, and understanding of the other family members, for example the changes around the arrival of a new baby.

Problems within the family system develop when it loses its ability to respond flexibly to changed circumstances but remains stuck at an inappropriate stage. Such difficulties might emerge at the outset – failure of the new system to develop appropriate ways of managing their emotional ties to their parents. Or at other times in the family's existence – the reader can no doubt think of many life crises that demand that a family suddenly change and adapt such as: loss of a grandparent; illness of a child; move to a new town; spouse beginning to work following a career break etc.

Parallels with this developmental model can be drawn in education. No doubt there would be a diversity of view as to what exactly comprises appropriate adaptation at each stage but the following is offered as a possible outline:

Stage	Appropriate functioning of pupil–teacher system as working towards
Nursery stage	Teacher enabling and encouraging the development of cooperative activity with many children of the same age.
Primary stage	Teacher promoting a system where pupils learn by self-discovery, partnership, group and whole-class activities, with the teacher acting as a resource for pupil learning.
Secondary stage	Teacher making more explicit work performance demands as pupils are guided towards the achievement of particular goals.
FE/6th form stage	A phase of self-directed learning with much more onus upon the learner. The teacher playing the part of enabler/facilitator.

Once a stage model is developed then clearly there are particular demands and expectations at each given stage. Where expectations are not met or are mismatched then problems will develop. This is most readily seen in the upper years of secondary school, years 4 and 5, where some of the pupils face the conflicting demands of being young adults outside school, but directed learners within it.

Where pupils and/or teachers fail to meet each others' expectations then difficulties develop. Parents invited in to hear about such difficulties can often express surprise, saying such things as 'Well he was never any trouble at primary school', conveying their confusion as to their child's and their own need to adapt to the demands of the very different secondary system.

Chapter 4

Systems as structures or structures as systems?

Some systemic thinkers reject the notion that there are given and appropriate structures within systems. In other words they feel that there are no appropriate models or expectations but that each system is self-determined by the participants within it. When such a system gets 'stuck' and becomes dysfunctional then the worker's task is simply to help the participants define the system's new direction.

There is a complex and rewarding philosophical debate as to whether the new deconstructurist approach is the way forward for society as a whole. The author feels that the outcome of this debate lies a good way off and has therefore sought to apply and develop an approach that seems most relevant and pragmatic for current use in schools. Given that in many families and in most schools, there are authority-hierarchical structures and that behavioural referrals develop when these are challenged, an approach that conceptualises systems in such structural terms seems to be the most attractive option.

This structural approach was drawn from the work of Minuchin. Minuchin has worked and developed his approach in very challenging family contexts and has been willing to openly explore its usefulness and relevance for people. Recently he has widened his field of intervention to include large scale systems. Those interested in pursuing Minuchin's ideas at depth may care to follow his publications in chronological order (1974–1984). For those who are simply interested in acquiring a flavour of his thinking then the author particularly recommends *The Family Kaleidoscope* (1984).

Data gathering

Minuchin argues that the best way of understanding a troubled system is to experience it. In this sense he worked to experience the family's difficulty to secure a better understanding. Such a style of working is known as the 'current process model'. The approach is not archeological, that is it does not ask what the long-term history attached to this system is. Rather it asks what the current difficulties portrayed by it are. This focus on the 'here and now' is very attractive as it frees the worker from exploring the developing history of the problem. In exploring the problem Minuchin advocated sampling the difficulty directly through interaction with that system.

Within a family therapy practitioner context this was achieved by:

Observation	The direct viewing of the family's ongoing interaction.
Enactment	Asking the family to repeat an example of their dysfunctionality.
The use of non-verbal communication	The workers, through their monitoring of the session, seeing and making explicit the communication that has been implicit within the session.

In relating this form of thinking to working in an educational setting, certain assumptions were challenged and established practices changed. In other words the author was able to switch to a 'what can be seen in the interaction now' approach and away from a long detailed case history gathering task. Problem behaviours are rarely single one-off events, rather they develop over time. A great deal of effort and energy can then be spent in exploring this history with the participants concerned. Many practitioners recommend just such an approach and the author certainly used it as an aspect of his initial fieldwork practice. One inevitable outcome is that staff offer a view of the difficulty as being the changing presentation of the problem as evinced by the pupil's reported behaviour. Whilst this may afford some insight into the past difficulties and convey a flavour of the redundant effort that has been made to solve a problem, time can be better spent in finding out about the difficulties as they are experienced today. Indeed today's interaction, as shown by the way that elements in the system transact, provides the richest source of information about the problem. Information is sought about the interaction between the participants in as many of the subsystems as possible that are engaged with the referred individual.

At the outset this approach conceptualises the problem in a different and creative way. In gathering data through interaction with the subsystems the worker assumes that all the participants are at any one time trying their best. This is known as working from the 'no blame' position. The worker assumes that if the participants could have found a better way to interact with each other they would have done so. In approaching the problem from the 'no blame' position the worker tries not to enter into a coalition or an alliance with anyone, thereby retaining the ability to be accepted by all the participants as a valid support. The worker aims to gather sufficient information to be able to:

— understand the problem;
— challenge all the systems members;
— shift their perceptions of the problem.

In attempting this type of intervention the workers are not conveying a moral or judgmental attitude that says 'You are wrong/doing things badly.' Rather they try to communicate that, together, there can be other and different ways of doing things. The workers attempt to understand the problem in structural terms. Minuchin in describing family structures (1974) stated that they can be seen in 'The invisible use of functional demands that organises the ways in which family members interact.'

Within a family, the nature of the subsystem within which an individual functions gets defined by its transactional patterns. In these patterns can be seen the different and differing levels of authority that parents and children have within their families. It is Minuchin's view that, to be effective, parents need to be able to transact with their children with appropriate authority. The nature of this authority and the way in which it is communicated, will change over time as the family moves through its various developmental tasks.

This can be seen in the way in which a parent's authority is conveyed very differently when dealing with a three-year-old as compared with a fifteen-year-old. This authority is not 'held' solely by the parent, it is part 'given' by the child. When children cease to give authority to their parents there may be a crisis and a sudden departure from home.

A similar pattern operates in school where teachers have at least three types of authority:

Role authority   I am a teacher you are a pupil.

Expert authority   I know a great deal about this subject and can convey it well.

Social authority   I know that you, as a pupil, have contracted to allow me a degree of authority over you.

John Robertson (1989) has articulated these ideas in his book *Effective Classroom Control*. Clearly, most teachers rely on expert and social authority in their transactions with pupils but when they feel forced to use their role/power authority to secure or maintain control then things often go wrong.

Authority and boundaries

Minuchin developed the concept of appropriate boundaries between the levels of a hierarchy. These are illustrated in Figure 14 below.

– – – – – – – – – A clear boundary where the adults are accessible to the children but not children with them.

•••••••••••••••• An enmeshed boundary where the boundary between the adult and child is unclear and the adults and children occupy poorly defined positions.

━━━━━━━━━━ A disengaged boundary which shows rigidity where the adult and child are totally out of reach of each other.

Figure 14   Minuchin's three boundaries

In parental activity terms this might be echoed by the following three scenarios.

Scenario 1
Where a father plays a game with his children with enthusiasm and enjoyment but is able to mark that there are rules to be followed if the game is to work.

Scenario 2
Where a father not only plays with the children with enthusiasm but, when someone cheats, starts to cheat as well. When the quarrelling starts the father and the children argue in the same childlike way.

Scenario 3
Where a father refuses to play a game with the child, such as cricket, but goes to watch a county match without taking the child. Even where there seems to be a common interest the adult remains detached and only involved in adult things.

Minuchin developed a diagrammatic schema for describing family structures in order to provide some clarity and understanding as shown in Figure 15 below:

Parents	**F**	**=**	**Father**
	M	**=**	**Mother**
Children	**C1**	**=**	**Eldest**
	C2	**=**	**and so on**

Figure 15

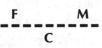

Figure 16

Figure 16 shows a family where there is an appropriate boundary between the parents and the child.

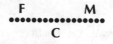

Figure 17

Figure 17 shows a family where the parents have become enmeshed with the child and start to lose the adult position, for example where parents engage in a slanging match with a child; or where parents fight the child's battle with his peers in the same childlike way etc. Note that enmeshed parents are not 'bad' parents. Their motivation is not necessarily in question, rather it is their 'position' that contributes to the problem.

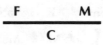

Figure 18

Figure 18 shows a disengaged family where the parents are relatively uninvolved with the child. Sometimes this is mistakenly caricatured along social class lines with the idea that 'Dad spends all his time down the pub and Mum goes to bingo.' Such behaviour does not necessarily indicate disengaged parenting since in the times that they are within the home the adults may be very accessible to the child. It is equally possible to imagine it being true of a 'very successful couple' who are both actively pursuing their own careers and career development. This may leave them little time, energy or emotion for parenting.

Within family systems Minuchin introduced a series of other concepts that helped depict the transactions taking place – see Figure 19.

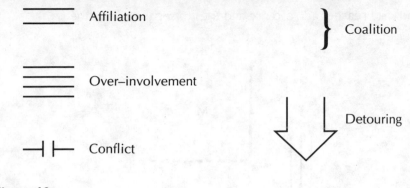

Affiliation

Coalition

Over–involvement

Detouring

Conflict

Figure 19

The following examples might help to illustrate some of these ideas . . .

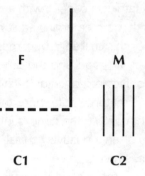

F   M

C1   C2

Figure 20

Figure 20 may well describe a mother's over-involvement with her second child. This may have been the result of a complex or difficult birth or the fact that this is a 'precious' child born to a couple in their early forties and long after the mother had given up hope of a second child. Such a system may cope reasonably well whilst the father and the first born can sustain an effective relationship. However, taken to extremes, the mother may become so protective of the younger child that she over-involves herself in the child's every action and decision. The second child may respond by meeting all of her mother's emotional needs but in doing so fails to meet her own – the result may be an emotional paralysis.

Both father and the first born child may experience this over-involvement as an alienation and rejection of them. Such difficulties may emerge dramatically when the family struggle to accommodate to the transition towards another stage of functioning, for example when the second child reaches adolescence and tries to separate from the mother.

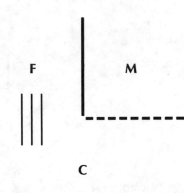

Figure 21

Figure 21, again, shows father in conflict with a child. It is quite a common feature of adolescence that the emerging adult challenges the parental view of the world. Sometimes this challenge becomes a split one, where one parent is characterised as 'all good' and the other as 'all bad'. This channels the adult–adolescent conflict into one adult–child dyad. This can be seen as a normal stage in a family's maturity but where the adult and child get locked into repeated redundant conflict, the family's integrity is put at risk. The subject of the conflict is often a relatively trivial one, for example, the time when the young person is meant to come in at night. However, this is only the chosen site for a much more serious conflict. Programmes like PET (Parent Effectiveness Training, 1970) try to help adults see that there are other more productive ways of dealing with such issues.

Figure 22

There are occasions when one parent may develop an alliance or coalition with a child in order to deal with a particular issue or problem with their spouse – see Figure 22. One example might be where the mother becomes concerned at the amount of time and family resources the father spends in

54

the local pub. In time, the mother and child may form an expert coalition against the father. This may take the form of accusations and challenges about his behaviour and demands that he spends more time in home-directed activities. Such demands may be balanced with an equal resistance and the two sides dig in and reinforce their given positions. The family may survive in this situation until their interaction is challenged by some crisis, such as loss of a job, child leaving home, illness within the family etc. Such an event challenges them to give up their entrenched positions, but these may have become so rigidified that they are unable to do so.

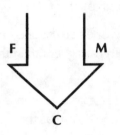

Figure 23

The scenario of Figure 23 is often beautifully depicted in situation comedies. At its most absurd it is portrayed as a family dialogue that runs something like this:

Mother (*To son about father who is sat in the same room.*) Jonathan will you please tell your father his dinner is ready and on the table.
Father (*Not looking up and not acknowledging that direct communication with his wife is possible.*) Jonathan will you please tell your mother I will eat when I'm ready and not before.

This is an overt example of a conflict being re-routed through the child who then becomes the transmitter of both sets of parental communications. However, such conflict can be conducted in many more subtle ways that are less readily seen but which can prove pernicious and harmful, particularly to the child who becomes the stress bearer of the parental battle.

One instance might be where a parent decides to return to work after a career break lasting until the children start secondary school. Father may feel, but is unable to say, that this suggests that he has not provided a good enough home for the family and that his wife has been forced to become the joint provider. Equally, the mother may be unable to describe her own anxieties about returning to work – her own self-doubt as to whether she can survive the transition back to employment. This inability to share the real problem may become diverted through a dialogue with the child where the father may expound strong views about neglect and the latchkey child, whilst the mother speaks of wanting to earn some money so that their child can have the same as all the other lads.

The child, receiving both communications, experiences the emotional tension between the parents and has to carry this split view. If the tension becomes too great he may act out the tension through misbehaviour, such as failing with schoolwork, truancy, staying out late etc. In turn, both parents may see this behaviour as a justification of their given position:

Father   Well no wonder now she's abandoned him to go back to work.
Mother   He's had to cope with having less than the other kids and now he's
          making us pay for it.

They would find it difficult to see that their son is providing them with something different to worry about so that they can stop quarrelling with each other through him.

The four examples outlined above provide details of the kind of family systems that the diagrams might be illustrating. In each instance at least one of the adults has lost the adult position and has become inappropriately involved with the child.

Over a two-year period the author tried to develop a way of using the same concepts to understand referred problems of behavioural difficulty that were being described as intractable or unchangeable in school. Minuchin's ideas of boundary and hierarchy have been adapted to describe the pupil–teacher–parent system.

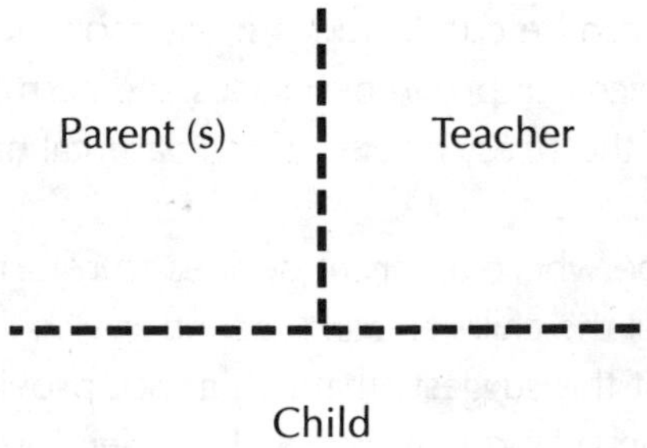

Parent (s)   Teacher

Child

Figure 24

Figure 24 might be considered to be an idealised view of the pupil–teacher–parent system. Both teacher and parent(s) are in the adult level of the hierarchy and are accessible to each other in their given roles. This may mean the teacher informing the parent about the child's progress in school and the parent informing the teacher of any relevant developments at home – things that might affect the child's behaviour in school. Both adults, in their respective roles, are available for and accessible to the child.

It is easy to suggest that if matters were depicted as in Figure 25 below, then problems might develop.

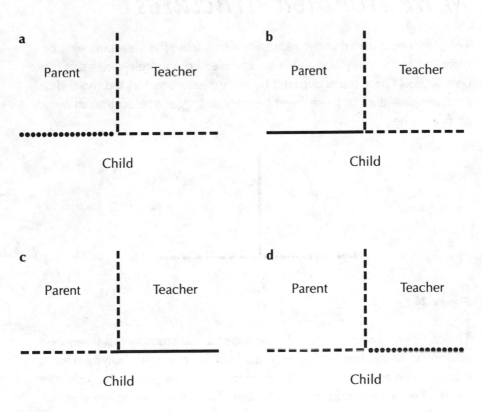

Figure 25

Reader may care to take this opportunity to check their understanding of the idea of structures and boundaries by:

1. Writing a few short notes to describe the diagrams in structural terms.
2. Considering what this might mean in terms of difficulties that might emerge in school.

Bear in mind that the diagram might refer to a multiplicity of possible scenarios.

Having done this please turn to Appendix 2, page 124 to check your understanding and to read a short example which illustrates each diagram. Please remember that the diagram might depict the structure in a number of referred situations but the interactions and enactment of these problems will be unique to each system.

More troubled structures

The scenarios outlined above represent a shift from the ideal but might be regarded as commonplace within the complex composite systems that make up a school. The systems depicted below are less common and more clearly problematic – each of these might be likely to trigger a referral to an outside agency for help.

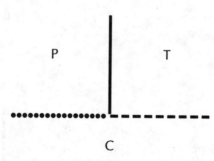

Figure 26

The complex example (Figure 26) describes a real situation that developed where a child had been referred by a school for persistent bullying. This proved to be a multi-layered and entrenched referral where the parents and the teacher were at odds with each other. The parents were vehement in their view that their child was being unfairly treated by the teacher, that there were plenty of other children who hit out in school. In their view Graham, their son, was being victimised. Furthermore, as it was a school in a rough area to which they had moved some two years before, they felt that Graham needed to learn to stand up for himself.

The teacher experienced the parents as aggressive and hostile and felt that this clearly explained Graham's behaviour in school (and that the problem was genetic!). As both parents refused to see anything wrong with their son there was no chance he would change and so would need to be taught somewhere else.

Both sets of adults were exasperated with each other and had resorted to communication, at best, at arms length and, at worst, through Graham. The worker, in joining this system, was able to see the parents' behaviour as emotional over-involvement. Furthermore, when this surfaced in public, in the presence of his friends, Graham was clearly made uncomfortable by it. Given this clear understanding of the problem and the necessary skills to work with each element of it, then the prognosis for positive change improved.

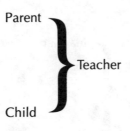

Figure 27

In many respects Figure 27 might provide a clear illustration as to where the problem above might deteriorate without some kind of resolution. In this scenario both parents and child have joined in a coalition against the teacher. The problem may begin with the parents openly discussing that the teacher is wrong and that they intend to tell him so. At the outset the child may simply witness this discussion and only gradually participate in it. However, over time, with or without their active encouragement, the child may take it upon himself to actively represent their opposition by such classroom comments as, 'My old man says its nothing to do with you what happens with me and my mates.' Such a complex problem is unresolvable by focusing upon the child as this will simply add to the circularity of the communication.

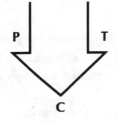

Figure 28

Figure 27 showed what may happen when the child and parents are in an active coalition against the teacher. In Figure 28 the child has become the conduit for detoured conflict between home and school. Such a situation might arise over the management of homework. Parents, unsympathetic to education following their own poor school experiences, may express the view that the child should learn in school and that the work is the teacher's responsibility. The teacher feels that the parents should be making greater effort to see that homework is done as their child is potentially very able. This conflict either covertly or overtly gets detoured through the child who feels the tension of having to choose between two sets of adults who claim to be showing care for him. Faced with making such an impossible choice the child starts to act out his confusion through misbehaviour.

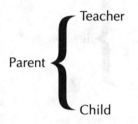

Parent { Teacher / Child

Figure 29

Figure 29 depicts teacher and child joined in a coalition against parents. One example where this developed, despite all the best of intentions, began when a teacher felt that a child was showing signs of neglect in school. The pupil arrived in school unwashed, unkempt and generally unhygienic. Liking the child, but offended by her appearance, the teacher made the mistake of exploring the problem with the child in terms that suggested it was not her fault but rather the shortcomings of her home. This allowed the teacher to keep the teacher–pupil dyad intact but the outcome was that the child returned home that day to announce, 'Mrs Thomas says you two just don't care enough about me.' The result was a total fracturing of the relationship between home and school.

Since the teacher did not deal directly with the parents, nor teach self-help skills to the child, nor contact another, more appropriate agency, it proved difficult to reinvent a viable home–school subsystem at all.

The author hopes that the worked examples show how drawing a conceptual map of the problem in systems terms aids understanding. Having gained such understanding, the obligation lies with the worker to plan an effective intervention that helps to redefine the existing hierarchy with appropriate viable boundaries. This means working with pupil, teachers and parents to help them move towards more appropriate, functionally viable positions. The techniques for enabling such change and the process of promoting it form the substance of the next chapter.

Chapter 5

Systems thinking within school pastoral interventions

As has been mentioned before, the pastoral referral system in schools can often find that it gets choked with return business. It has been a much repeated complaint of pastoral colleagues that they spent a hugely disproportionate amount of their time in seeing the same young people, over the same kind of problem, throughout the school year. Is the referred young person truly bad? Has everyone else who is involved fulfilled their responsibilities? Or is the problem simply being passed on to the head of year out of habit?

In a sense, the reason matters less than the fact that the constant re-referral suggests that there is circularity taking place. The head of year referral has moved from being a significant *point of punctuation* in the cycle to simply being an aspect of what systems thinkers call '*more of the same*'.

Initially, the head of year may feel gratified by this type of referral (after all, we all need to be needed). Such referrals reinforce our sense of self and enable us to feel effective and significant within school. The key question, however, is just how much of this load can one person or even one pastoral team be realistically expected to carry?

One possible scenario is that the referral system becomes so autocratic that it reaches overload. Perhaps the best illustration of how absurd this can become was where, during an in-service day, one head of year complained about this very difficulty. In his school it had become custom and practice for troubled pupils to be referred to him even when he was teaching. Worse still he taught chemistry. At its worse he could find that he had two or even three troublesome pupils sent from other classes seated at the back of his classroom, which was a busy working laboratory. Being a resilient, durable personality, this head of year had gone on coping with this situation for some years. Even so, his concern at the position in which he found himself was quite evident, coupled perhaps with too little sense of the 'risk' to which such practices put his own position.

The ultimate end point of carrying too much of the load leads to what might be called the 'pastoral double bind'. A double bind is when someone signals one message whilst clearly giving a second and contradictory message. In this instance it begins with referral of troublesome pupils to a head of year. The head of year generates a response – without clear guidelines to work from due to the paucity of training in this field. Such a response often has to be self-invented. These responses are a matter of trial and error until one finds something that proves effective. Initially the pupil may respond by returning to class somewhat chastened. (Note that the intervention back in the classroom may be unchanged.)

The teacher making the referral tells his/her colleagues of the head of year's impact and they too make referrals to 'test' the system. Initially gratified that his colleagues are beginning to rely upon him, the head of year repeats his 'act' with a number of pupils. As the rate of referral increases (in a busy school it will always feel that there are more problems than solutions) these heads of year find that they are working hard against a gathering tide of work. There is too little time to plan an individual response and so they readily reach for the strategy/strategies that have worked before. Given the pace of the work, they inadvertently finds themselves repeating the same performance with the same pupils. (A clear example of contributing to circularity.) The only thing that changes is that the pupil may on this occasion feel less chastened and so may be re-referred to the head of year even sooner.

It can be seen that this is not now a *cycle* of referral but a steadily tightening *spiral* of referral. To try to manage this the heads of year work faster – spending less time and attention upon each referral. Some compensate for this by trying to make greater impact, often by conducting the encounter at high volume. As a spectator to such encounters it is often possible to watch the teacher and pupil engage in the dance together: The pupil appears at the door with a total body language that says 'I'm here for more again.' The head of year – again non-verbally – says 'Oh no not you *again*!' Reluctantly, both partners begin the dance, each expecting it to prove less than satisfactory, yet each expecting to be dancing again in a little while!

The pastoral double bind

The head of year now seems to be severely tied up within what can be termed the 'pastoral double bind'. The contradictory messages read something like this:

Classteacher (to head of year)	You are a very experienced problem solver in school. I have an unresolved problem with a pupil in my class. Please solve this problem on my behalf.

If the referral succeeds then by implication the problem was *solvable*. The classteacher can now feel relieved that the problem no longer exists,

Classteacher (to head of year)	You've succeeded – well, no wonder, you have so much more free time than us.

However, if the problem has not been resolved by the encounter then the communication is:

Classteacher (to head of year)	You've failed – so what *do* you do with all that time?

Clearly this is a caricature of an exchange carried to its extreme but unless the interaction back in the classroom becomes a focus for the referral then the problem is likely to re-emerge.

What can the heads of year do? In a busy school drawing its pupils from an area with a matrix of socio-economic need there will always be demands made upon committed members of staff. Faced with an increasing workload, coupled with a sense of deepening under-performance, the heads of year have to cut the workload or distance themselves from it. The first may be achieved by referral on to:

– the deputy headteacher
– the headteacher

and ultimately outside agents:

– the educational psychologist
– the education social worker
– the child guidance clinic etc.

The second response may be apparent where the head of year loses his zest for the task and begins to convey an attitude of 'Well what can you expect of such kids?'

Failure to find a way out of the tightening spiral can result in increased stress levels with consequent tension, absenteeism, illness etc. It may be that as the gap between what their colleagues expect of them and what can be achieved widens, it becomes unbridgeable and they may develop *burn out* Fruggeri (1990).

Clearly this is an unsatisfactory process with problems being left unresolved, or decanted onto someone or somewhere else, or staff being worn down by the unrelenting pressure of it all as reported by the Elton Committee on: *Discipline in Schools* (1989). Can systemic thinking make any kind of contribution to our understanding and thereby enhance our responses to such problems? If we return to our systems map we construed the ideal teacher–parent–pupil system as that shown in Figure 30. Let us assume that a problem starts to develop within the classroom. The teacher identifies a given pupil as being the cause/pivot of the problem. Unwittingly the teacher responds to the problem in a way that reinforces the significance of the pupil, say, by exchanging verbal banter, then sarcasm, only to find that the pupil is extremely accomplished at this and even seems to enjoy it. We then have a system that looks like the one in Figure 31. The teacher has now become enmeshed with the pupil and discovers that he is engaged in what amounts to an argument/quarrel with the pupil. In doing this, he has jeopardised his own authority and is losing the adult position in the way that he is interacting with the pupil. Notice that it is something that has just happened; the teacher is not blamed for this development. If one were working from a blaming position it is equally easy to blame the boy by saying that he used inappropriate provocative language at the outset. In systems terms the issue is 'What is the transaction now?'

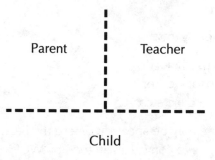

Parent | Teacher

Child

Figure 30

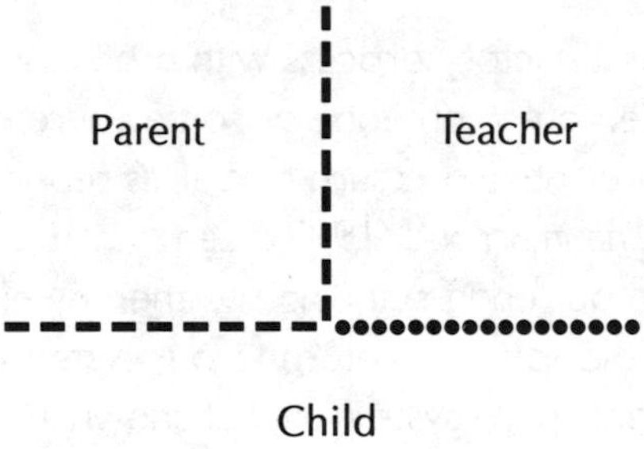

Parent | Teacher

Child

Figure 31

Since this is a secondary school, it is quite unlikely that a classteacher would make direct contact with the parents. Appropriate availability and access between classteacher and parents might be considered to be through a forum such as a parents evening or open day. In the classroom, the teacher becomes quite anxious as to where this interaction may lead, and how it might escalate, and therefore seeks support from the head of year.

Given the busy places that schools are, and the all too congested timetable, the head of year may respond by simply seeing the pupil. If the problem proves to develop beyond the scope of this response then he may determine that he needs to speak to the parents, with or without the pupil being present. It is somewhat unlikely that he will decide that the classteacher will also need to be present at such an encounter.

If we re-examine the position within the structural framework the head of year has intended to move in alongside the teacher and support him or her in the management of the referred pupil (see back to Figure 29); the head of year tries to support the teacher through managing the contact with the parent. In practice these actions may have given clear messages that add to the problem:

To the pupil   He/she has communicated a confirmation that his classteacher cannot control him.

To the parents   He/she has communicated that the classteacher cannot manage a direct transaction with them. Worse still, some parents, unsympathetic to the school, may construe the absence of the classteacher as the school having something to hide!

To the teacher   He/she has confirmed the idea that this is not his problem now – but it has become a referral that the head of year has made his/her own.

The likely prognosis is far from that of a positive outcome. The pupil feels empowered in his relationship with the teacher. He is confirmed in his belief that he can cause difficulties for a competent adult professional. The parents may feel that they are only being given a part story. They have tackled their son about the matter and it is quite clear that the classteacher is not blameless. In fact they may be quite unhappy with the teacher about some of the exchanges that their son has had in the classroom (direct quotation out of context and out of sequence can certainly flavour the impression of an encounter).

The head of year has now committed his/her own ego and maybe that of the school in a declaration that the problem has to be solved and that things must change. This can hardly be seen as a positive position to begin to work towards a joint solution. The pupil has gained a sense of enhanced importance, the parents feel uncertain about the differing communication coming from their son and the school, and the teacher is primed to hand on the problem to the head of year as soon as it starts.

The intervention focused upon the pupil as being the problem. The head of year in managing the pupil as the problem, with the parents, on behalf of the teacher, has created the scenario depicted in Figure 32.

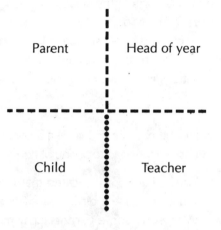

Figure 32

In systems terms he has entered the adult layer on behalf of, or in support of, the classteacher. As he handles the meeting with the parents by himself, the indirect message is that the teacher does not want to, or cannot manage, this transaction. The child sees his parents and the head of year manage the adult transaction whilst he, but most importantly the classteacher, gets told about it afterwards. The teacher has been displaced from the adult position, has been parented by the head of year and, as the diagram suggests, has joined the child level within the structure. Worse still, the real problem, the enmeshment of the interaction between teacher and pupil and pupil and teacher, has not been addressed. If anything, the enmeshment has been strengthened, with each of the dyad simply having access to other forms of extra help. Extra help for the teacher, in the form of the head of year, and for the pupil in the form of his parents.

At the outset, the head of year made the classteacher's problem his own. This is known as *owning the problem*. This is in itself an unsatisfactory concept as the head of year has only heard one half of the interaction at this point. Furthermore, now that he *owns the problem*, the head of year works hard to *solve the problem.* Even should he succeed through parental cooperation, pupil conformity and teacher performance, he has only managed a one-off solution. What is more, it is a one-off solution that the head of year *owns*. There has been no attempt to develop the skills of the classteacher and therefore he/she is no wiser when a similar difficulty emerges.

In working with the referred problem in the terms of its initial label, the head of year runs two clear risks:

    1.   The risk of *not skilling* or worse still of *deskilling* others.
    2.   The risk of creating *a dependency* relationship.

The argument suggests that the focus of the work should have been the enmeshment, that is the poor boundary between the teacher and the pupil (see Figure 33). To do this may require the head of year to work with the pupil *and* the teacher. If the worker had sufficient skills then it would help if he eventually worked with them together at the *same time*. This provides them with the opportunity to practise a new way of interacting together. This new enactment should enable them to establish a more effective appropriate boundary within their subsystem.

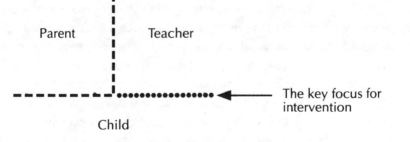

Figure 33

It may be that the shift or change can be helped by drawing upon success/ strength elsewhere in the system, for example the successful interaction of the pupil with his parents. This success is not used to manage the pupil but to provide a series of ideas as to how the teacher and the pupil might handle things differently. In making this strategic shift, there is more likelihood of achieving long-term success. As the head of year will not have taken sole ownership of the problem, he has simply tried to enable or facilitate the others in their working for change. Most importantly, at the point where change is achieved, the teacher and the pupil own the success for the change. This ensures that the improvement, as it has been defined by the participants, is likely to be more enduring and longlasting. Furthermore, the classteacher will have added to his classroom-coping strategies, will have gained significant skills beyond the delivery of his own academic subject, and will be better equipped to deal with the next challenge he faces.

It is apparent that in working this way the head of year is likely to spend significant time with those involved in the referral. However, this planned intensive response to a small number of chronic referred problems is likely to prove more effective and contribute significantly to the overall skills development of the staff. It seems unarguable that in a learning and learned profession, all should be committed to augmenting their personal skills.

It was a cause of regret to read the report by the Elton Committee on *Discipline in Schools* (1989) and fail to find a process model for addressing ways of dealing with entrenched school-based problems within it. If all staff are to gain from shared skills the means by which such gains are made needs to be clearly defined. This model provides a conceptual basis for such a process and should result in more broadly based behavioural management skills.

As the staff group become more effective in managing classroom-based difficulties, then the flood of referrals should slow to a trickle of entrenched and intractable cases that remain unresolved at classroom level. The busy practitioner in school may protest that this works well as an idea in the medium term, but how is the immediate short-term problem of the sheer quantity of referrals to be stemmed? The author would suggest in return that quality pastoral time is of far more use than quantity pastoral time. Focused, intensive effort, by key personnel is likely to bring more success than if they get sucked into day-to-day fire fighting.

How is the tide to be stemmed? In the first instance through the development of consistent ground rules and boundaries to protect the quality pastoral time. These can be developed by answering the following key questions:

What is the pastoral team for?
What is its core task?

In posing these questions with staff within schools and on in-service training days it has often become clear that the school has not developed a shared perspective as to what the team's key role is in the school. Even in quite troubled schools, where the pastoral system was clearly creaking under the strain, it was not unusual to hear 'checking registers' as a key task for those with the best developed interpersonal skills. However, in general, the focus of the pastoral task has been working with the factors that cause disaffiliation from school – behavioural difficulties and underfunctioning whilst on the other hand being proactive in developing programmes offering guidance in study skills and interpersonal relationships (see Hamblin, 1984).

In terms of responding to behavioural difficulties it is important that the pastoral team determines its boundaries and then manages them well with the rest of the staff. Teacher colleagues should receive a consistent and high quality service from their pastoral colleagues. This will enable them to develop coherent, realistic shared expectations as to what the pastoral team is trying to achieve.

Determining the boundaries for appropriate referrals is a useful activity to undertake with a staff group so that joint expectations are developed from the outset (good systemic practice). The following exercise has been an effective activity on in-service training days for helping staff to develop a dialogue to determine common practice.

Sorting the problem

There are seven instances of problem behaviour listed below. The information on each problem is very scant. In some cases we would all like to know more before we take a decision, in others the information may appear to be quite sufficient. For the sake of this activity accept the limited nature of the information and base your decisions upon it.

You are asked to read through the list of problems and then sort them into three levels of priority. First read the list of problems . . .

1. Janet keeps annoying the other fourth-year pupils around her.
2. Tim has come to school without any books, pens etc. again!

3. Michelle organised all the other fifth-year pupils to bang their desk lids midway through my lesson.
4. When told to get on with his work, Frank let rip with a torrent of abuse.
5. Marsha repeatedly gouges at her arm whenever I tell her what to do.
6. Graham simply refused to do any work.
7. Jean was chewing again.

Now re-read the list and label the problem as A, B or C.

A = Those problems that can and should be dealt with simply as a within-class problem. This means using those responses that every teacher might reasonably be expected to make.

B = Those that can be solved in the classroom plus. In other words, the sort of problem that a classteacher may reasonably be expected to manage – given the support of a listening ear and some ongoing expert guidance.

C = Those few but severe problems that cannot be solved in the classroom. Clearly they will require some help from the pastoral team out of and then back into the classroom.

(NB) Note that when withdrawing pupils because there are difficulties there should at the outset be a clearly agreed common agenda as to *when and how they are to return*. Equally the return should take the form of the classteacher reclaiming or regaining their 'adult position in the hierarchy'.

In getting a staff group to generate answers to this problem-sort activity, pastoral staff may gain a clear insight into the often different levels of expectation that their colleagues have of them.

The activity can be undertaken by individuals who can then work with one colleague to resolve any differences in their rating through discussion. Pairs can then meet with another pair to develop a common set of choices and so on. In this way the whole staff can develop a common determination of expectations both of themselves and the pastoral team. At this point the schools senior management team may have to arbitrate if the expectations are unreal or unattainable.

Naturally there is no right or wrong answer to such an exercise. Having used it extensively with small groups of staff from all of the comprehensive schools in one LEA the problem-sort categories on the next page represent their average view of the appropriate levels of referral. (My thanks to the colleague who said 'I bet we're writing his next book here', who saw the strength of the activity long before I did!)

Category A **Behaviour**

1. Jane keeps annoying other pupils.

7. Jean drawing again.

2. Tim in school without books and equipment again!

Category B **Behaviour**

2. Tim in school without books and equipment again! (split vote)

3. Michelle – banging desks.

Category C **Behaviour**

4. When told to get on with his work, Frank let rip with a torrent of abuse.

5. Marsha repeatedly gouging her arm.

6. Graham refusing to do any work.

For those who found this exercise useful for themselves, it may be worth considering using the activity with a staff team but listing problems that are felt to be relevant to their own school.

At its simplest level the activity can be used to define the boundaries and limits to referral. This, in itself, should limit the pastoral load and lead to enhanced practice. The activity can then be taken a stage further as a staff development exercise. Allocating staff into groups of four or five, each group is then given the designation letter A, B or C. As a group their task is to map out a series of strategies that might be employed to respond to the given problems. Often staff ask for more detailed information about each problem.

At this point, one response might be that they can add in any details they require, drawing upon their own classroom experiences i.e. they breathe life into the examples instead of receiving them from on high. The group is then asked to put their solutions in preferred rank order on an overhead transparency or flipchart paper.

After a full discussion has taken place (in my experience at least forty minutes) a spokesperson from each group presents their solution to the whole staff. At the end of each presentation the staff, as a whole, are given five to ten minutes to ask questions of the presenting group.

This activity produces many gains:

- It defines the limits to referral within the school.
- It develops a whole-school perception of problem behaviour.
- It enables less confident staff to engage in an open debate about ways of managing behaviour.
- It allows experienced colleagues who are 'too senior to train in behaviour management' to have the opportunity to hear a range of possible ideas and solutions.
- It may help in the development of a more 'open' culture, where staff can freely admit to having difficulties and can explore these problems with their peers in a spirit of supportive dialogue.

The activity is of equal value in working with heads of year to determine which problems they should:

- manage with the classteacher;
- tackle themselves;
- refer on up to the senior management;
- refer for outside help from a psychologist, social worker or clinic etc.

Whenever intervention is planned it is very important to define the boundaries of referral and responsibility so that everyone is aware of them.

Chapter 6

The skills of systems work

Engaging subsystems

The extent to which practitioners work with the subsystems around a
referred individual reflects their view of the problem. A balance has to be
struck between the totality of a young person's life and the available resource
to be committed towards developing a solution to that person's difficulties.

Beginnings

At the outset there is a need to meet with each subsystem that makes up
the problem and contains the potential solution. As the problem is being
expressed in school and is often seen as being the individual pupil, there is a
tendency for pastoral/support staff to meet with parents, teacher and pupil,
by appointment, in school. Such meetings, though convenient, may reduce
the amount of useful information available for the intervention and, more
importantly, may give specific messages to the participants.

In the case of an entrenched behavioural difficulty where parents may
have been summoned to school many times, to repeat such an invitation,
even with a wish to manage the encounter differently, will feel like more of
the same to the parents. It will be difficult to signal to them that this is a new
and fresh initiative. At other times it may be that where the referring
classteacher has been badly rattled by the behaviour of a child in class, he/she
may find it difficult if the matter were discussed by the head of year with the
parents and the pupil in their home first.

In effect, the order of the meetings, the venue chosen and the nature of the invitation to meet all convey messages about one's position and attitude to the problem. If the reader is a member of a pastoral team, then the first contact is likely to be with the referring teacher or teachers. There is a need to hear the problem clearly right through rather than just a snippet of it. However, such snippets like 'That James Baldwin's been a right little *so and so* in my lesson yet again!' convey a great deal about the level of the problem, its urgency and the degree of entrenchment likely to be faced in trying to get staff to take a fresh and positive view of it.

It is important to remember that you are hearing their subjective view of a recent and perhaps repeated event. Their anger, fear, frustration may all come through in talking about the behaviour of a pupil that seems to threaten their control. Such information is very helpful as it clearly indicates that as well as working towards changing James' actual behaviour, there is a need to help the referring teacher enhance his/her control in the classroom.

In listening to such information the author feels that it is important *not* to commit oneself in an alliance with the colleague against the pupil. There is a need to be seen to be willing to work in support of a colleague in difficulty. This needs to be from a balanced, informed position and not that of automatic, unthinking ally. If it is a stuck system, where no one person is to blame, there is a need to be supportive but not collusive. The author suggests that it is much more important to work to effect positive change and that this forms the truly supportive position to colleagues.

In deciding upon the point of entry, particularly to the parent–child or family subsystem, there are three possibilities:

- To meet at the school.
- To meet in the home.
- To meet at a third venue.

If the decision to meet at school is going to be seen as more of the same, then meet elsewhere, because if the parents have been to school a number of times with little positive result, then a further invitation is unlikely to be met with a fresh, positive and open response.

If allegations have been made by the parents, via the pupil, against the teacher, then there is a strong argument not to make initial contact via a home visit. It may inadvertently suggest that the school has something to hide. The use of a third venue can at times be very helpful in beginning anew.

This option largely depends upon the availability of such a premises within the community.

Try to make the invitation to meet as inclusive as possible. Invitations to meet with the teacher who has referred the problem in school may well convey a great deal of useful information. There is a need to balance this with information from other teachers who manage the class. It is unusual to discover that a pupil is a problem in absolutely every lesson he/she attends.

Invitations to parents are much more problematic. If the school has a history of only gaining access to one parent – and nothing has changed for the better through such contact – there is a good case for seeing *both* parents as part of your message that this is a different form of intervention and by implication will have a different outcome. The wording of such invitations is important; the use of standard school summoning letters is unlikely to help the process. Effective invitations are those that:

–   share the school's and the parents' *joint* concern;
–   stress that the parents have a positive role in promoting change;
    mark that the school is anxious to cooperate in such change;
–   emphasise that positive outcomes hinge upon effective open collaboration.

Dear Mr and Mrs Baldwin

As you are aware, James continues to experience difficulty in settling to work in the classroom.

You must be very concerned that his difficulties get resolved as soon as possible. I am sure that you will be as anxious to help improve things for James, as we are in school. Together we can be effective in helping him learn to settle in class.

With this in mind I would like us to meet and am suggesting Friday, 11 November, at 1.30 p.m. If there are any problems with this arrangement perhaps you might ring and let me know?

Yours sincerely

The only difficulty with such an approach is that it assumes that the family is literate and able to respond to such an invitation. It may be that the welfare officer has to make such an invitation in person. If so, there is a need to ensure that the positive message is still confidently conveyed.

The invitation becomes much more problematic when those parenting the child are in a non-formalised relationship and only one of them is a natural parent. In systems terms this is the subsystem that the pupil participates in for the bulk of his life, and not to positively engage all elements of it may result in key information being missed and powerful support for change being ignored. The aim of the initial overture must be:

—　to work to effect change;
—　to be most effective in that work – that is do not do other people's jobs, such as being classteacher/parent to the child;
—　to maximise the impact of the work through the minimal input necessary to secure change;
—　to work in a way that empowers others – so that it is *their* problem and *their* solution, as this allows you to make a successful withdrawal.

These statements all seem very straightforward and it is hard to disagree with the sentiments that they express. However, it requires much concentration and attention to detail to translate these ideas into effective practice.

The paragraphs below illustrate how inadvertently one can reinforce the message to teachers that a pupil was the product of a truly problematic family and that the responsibility for change was not theirs. In conveying such a message the intervention gets impaired. For a long-established problem to change, there is a need for the pupil to experience different management from his parents. Even if this change is secured, it is unlikely to have impact in school unless the teachers actively signal that they, too, expect support and at times insist upon change. The paragraph forms a short extract adapted from a longer letter to all James' teachers. Read the text and see if you can determine where it makes systemic errors.

Dear Colleague

I am working with the psychologist, as a support teacher to try to help James Baldwin. I will be in the school Monday to Thursday from 11.00 a.m.–12.00 p.m. Initially James will be seen on a one-to-one basis.

James has made a commitment to change his behaviour. To help him, James' parents have agreed to link the level of his pocket money with his reported behaviour in school. The head of year and I will maintain contact with the parents. James' parents will record and sanction bad behaviour and record and reward good behaviour.

The problems are now so entrenched that the family are unlikely to succeed without the support of the school.

Clearly where staff have repeatedly experienced difficulties with a pupil the signal to them is that despite the involvement of a support teacher matters are so bad at home that the likelihood of lasting change is remote.

Joining

Minuchin and Fishmann (1981) describe this as a specific set of skills. It means experiencing the people as they are together; the pace, volume and nature of their communication together. Much can be learned about the potential for change from this less active but very attentive stage of an intervention.

In *joining* with a teacher colleague/colleagues to hear about the referred problem it is important to listen to what is being said and to what is left unsaid, *but* most important of all is the *way* in which things are being said. In meeting with teacher and pupil together, much can be learned quickly from the way in which they both describe the problem in the classroom. Similarly, when meeting with the parent–pupil or family subsystem, much can be readily learned from the way in which:

1. The family places itself. Who sits next to whom? Is the pupil using his mother/father for protection? Is a parent comforting/reassuring the child? Is the pupil sat apart from the parents and detached from them?
2. How the group sits. Who is turned away from whom? Who is tight and tense and finding this difficult? Who is ignoring/rejecting this encounter?
3. Who speaks. Not only who talks on behalf of the subsystem, but who is taking responsibility for it.

Much of this can be seen very quickly in the first few minutes of an encounter. Clearly if one parent is very enmeshed with the pupil — arguing and squabbling with him/her — then this is useful information in trying to plan for change.

It is sometimes hard to keep track of all that is going on, especially when someone is describing the problem, or past difficulties or the responses that they have tried to make to date. However, it is essential that one tries to tune into the *process* — the way in which the members of this subsystem interact together — rather than focusing solely on the *content* of what is said. An example might help to highlight this more clearly.

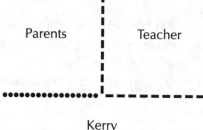

Figure 34

The author was asked to help with a pupil whose problems were located as being in the home. Kerry was fifteen years old and had been truanting regularly for some time. Recently he had appeared in school, somewhat inebriated, and had broken a glass panel in a door. The school was concerned that the parents should have help since Kerry's father was trying to establish a small mobile retail shop and his mother had recently collapsed and been admitted to hospital.

Father and son came to the first session. Father had come from work, while Kerry was in casual clothes — jeans and a leather jacket. The room was warm and Kerry hung the jacket on the door. Father explained the problem as Kerry

- sniffing glue and aerosols;
- truanting;
- messing about;
- being drunk in school;
- laughing all the time.

Once underway father had a seemingly endless list of complaints against his son. Most of them were minor, but some appeared to be of very high-risk behaviour. His manner and attitude was very rejecting of Kerry – regularly repeating 'He'll have to go somewhere else to live just like his brother.'

Kerry seemed bored by the episode as if he had heard it all before. He seemed to be uninterested in his past catalogue of misdemeanours and did not challenge/repudiate his father's version of events.

After about fifty minutes the session began to close with seemingly little positive information to work with. Father seemed quite prepared to send his son away and Kerry appeared to be indifferent to his father's threats. As they prepared to leave, father stood, collected his son's jacket off the hook and handed it to him. The gesture was warm, caring and entirely at odds with the negative things he had said about his son. This single piece of interaction provided critical information for subsequent work – but without the discipline of consciously paying attention to their interaction, it would have been missed.

In joining, whether with the parental or the school-based subsystem, it is important to try to retain a degree of objectivity. Having listened at length to an angry teacher describing an incident, or to an angry parent complaining about the way their child is being dealt with in school, there is a need to have listened and to demonstrate that you accept their concerns. This does not mean colluding with them against the other parties involved as this will prevent you from working effectively with all of the subsystems as you will be seen as being allied with one party. In effect this means being able to be aware of, but not an integral part of, the transaction within the subsystem. To observe the nature of the interaction in a detached manner so as to be in a position to use this information for effective change.

This is a very difficult role to play – to gain acceptance by all concerned as an enabler of change – whilst not alienating any particular party. This means performing the 'credible ritual' of being an education-based professional whose involvement stems from a concern to get matters improved in school.

In listening to teacher colleagues describe a pupil as being 'the problem', it is important to listen, whilst not colluding with them as being the only party with a valid viewpoint. This would confirm that the situation is unchangeable and that they, the teachers, do not have to work for a better outcome. It is essential that empathy for a colleague does not work to prevent you enabling them to contribute to positive change.

When working with parents and pupils many attempt to use Christian names and it is tempting to take this as a mark of acceptance. However, if the convention of the school is that staff are addressed more formally, then the credible ritual is not being maintained. Worse still the pupil may carry this informality back into school and jeopardise the worker's credibility with teacher colleagues.

Pace

In joining with the subsystems it is possible to understand the pace of the interactions within them and the degree to which these interactions have become entrenched. The speed with which the members of the subsystem transact with each other helps to define the pace of the worker's involvement with them. Moving too quickly often results from one's own need to be seen to be actively effective in getting change – or even just to be doing something!

Where problems have become entrenched and are long established, their resolution is unlikely to be rapid if it is to be long lasting. The need to move too quickly can stem from our own need to be effective, something the author calls being the cherished professional, an issue explored in the section on advice. There is a need to act and to act appropriately. If the participants are engaged and are willing to support change then any delay in initiating change will result in a loss of momentum and a degree of disillusion with the initiative. One must always remember that people will already have tried to solve the difficulty at least once.

Observing and listening

Working with a problem of the use of foul language by a pupil in a classroom, the author once invited the parents and the pupil to a meeting at the school. The pupil was thirteen years old and only swore in practical lessons. Parents and pupil arrived together and I restated the reason for our meeting. To my amazement I only had to ask what the group thought of the problem and the session took off. It became apparent that the parents actively blamed each other and as their discussion continued, each demonstrated their skill in quoting the other's improper use of language. At times the pupil would confirm one parent's allegation against the other. She, the pupil, seemed to be trying to be fair and offered confirmation to both of them.

The speed of their speech, the volume of their exchanges and the fact that all three could quite happily talk at once in the presence of a stranger, was useful and evident within ten minutes of the meeting beginning. This episode was a useful encounter as it became clear that, having been with the group, there was a definite need for some rules of transaction in order to manage the session towards a positive outcome. The key rules to use in this situation were that:

– everyone had to speak for themselves;
– only one person was to be speaking at any one time;
– everyone could have the chance to speak before someone spoke twice.

Even with these rules agreed, the pace of this particular group's communication remained very fast.

Seeing it as it is

When working with the school or the home subsystem it can appear as if the problem is getting confused with the person. For example, in describing a problem, a teacher might say, 'He just storms into class, dumps himself in his seat declaring he will be doing no work.' Or a pupil might complain 'Even when I've just come in and sat down the teacher's after me.' They may both be describing the same incident or a whole series of incidents. In trying to determine who is correct the worker may risk alienating the other party. Far better to ask the pair to show you exactly what they mean (a) about the other's behaviour, and (b) about their own behaviour.

This *enacting* of the problem can often result in a clearer definition of the difficulty, with participants almost haggling about the fine detail of the way in which someone sits down, closes a book, or even looks! Sometimes participants find it hard to enact a problem properly. This can be because they find it difficult to own and acknowledge the fact that they have contributed to the difficulty. However this, of itself, can effect change and there have been instances when the participants have themselves been able to see the complementarity of their behaviour. When both participants see for themselves how they contribute to the dance then things can change quickly.

At other times, it may be necessary to mark to the participants the ways in which they are maintaining each other's behaviour and to encourage them to invent a new or different way of dancing. The important issue is to ensure that it is they who determine the new steps and that they are not given by the worker. One example of this that worked well was when an exasperated head of year complained bitterly that he could not get one pupil's parents to acknowledge that their son was the cause of a number of problems in school. He spoke at length about his frustration with them and acknowledged that their unwillingness to see the boy as a contributor to the problem had now enlarged the matter in his own mind. Furthermore, he was now spending too much time and effort on it and felt the matter had to end. Having worked together before he was happy to accept the suggestion that we meet together with the parents to see if we could move matters forward.

At the meeting the parents and the head of year each described their view of events. The parents felt their son was one of many and that the problems were all small ones in which he was not the leader. The head of year was quite accusational and offered a pessimistic view of their son's future in the school. At which point the parents became quite angry.

The group was then asked to re-run as much of their last interview together as possible. After initial embarrassment and some stumbling, they managed what seemed like a fluent repetition of the meeting they had had before. Significantly the father, in the space of ten minutes, suggested that the problem was the result of:

— Others making him do it.
— Their son being with the wrong crowd.
— The boy genuinely forgetting that he had agreed to behave in a different, better way.

At this point we stopped and swapped seats. I asked the father to watch the encounter and tell us what was happening. I then tried to enact his role.

Once this second act closed, the father was asked for his comments. Reluctantly he offered the view that he hadn't been prepared to accept that his son was in any way to blame. He was then asked to comment on the head of year's performance. Having got over the novelty of this position, he finally managed to say, 'Well it always sounds like he's telling us off.'

We tried the scene again, this time with father being the head of year, trying to say things in a way that felt less critical of the parents. The outcome was a much improved communication between the adults and an agreed way of home and school working together. However, it was marked to all three that they would need to demonstrate their new open communication in the presence of the boy for it to be really effective.

Discussing the enactment afterwards, the head of year although pleased, felt that he himself could not have undertaken such a session alone. It was marked quite firmly with him that he could however offer the same support to his own pastoral colleagues in school, if such a problem emerged again.

Chapter 7

What to advise?

(This chapter draws heavily upon a paper drafted by two members of an intervention team who summarised the team's experience of giving advice in entrenched situations.)

One of the common difficulties encountered in primary schools stems from the fact that some children who exhibit difficult behaviour are saturated in goods and gifts. At times these come from the parents, but they can also be provided by grandparents and other members of the extended family.

A behavioural intervention based on withholding/rewarding treats/pocket money is unlikely to have impact in such circumstances. Advising parents that such munificence is not all that helpful is very difficult, particularly if it is their usual way of expressing regard or affection. More problematic still is when parents, embarrassed by their child's reported behaviour, respond with 'We've no idea why he's like this. We've given him everything that he's ever wanted. We've done everything that we could.' And sometimes unspoken, but often meant, 'We can't do any more'.

The wish to be positive and effective sometimes leads the worker into giving advice as to what can be done, but this can prove to be disastrous. Similarly, when supporting teacher colleagues, who ask 'So what is the answer then?' the temptation is to jump in with advice to justify our 'expertise'. The need to be needed and to be seen to be effective can result in many unforeseen problems.

The 'expert' professional

Early on in its work, one of the team, in supporting a teacher in the management of a troubled eight-year-old, had the following suggestions typed out:

The Following Might Prove Helpful in Your Management of Matthew

A reward system   A chart with prints/stars for good behaviour, as well as for good work. (We often forget to reward good behaviour and allow our attention to be drawn to the poor behaviour. Success can be rewarded with bigger stars, special activity, sending to other teachers or the headteacher, treats, letters home etc.)

Planned ignoring   Turn your attention to the others who are behaving well and praise the way they are working.

Use a *signal* agreed with Matthew beforehand that means 'Please stop at once'. Then reward him when successful.

Turn attention to something of interest to Matthew to divert him.

Enlist the support of the class who can help Matthew best overcome this problem.

If the group of children around Matthew become difficult to manage – *regroup* them.

In a team discussion the following week the support teacher expressed disappointment that she had found the note crumpled up on the classteacher's desk. It was much later when the worker redefined the problem, not as Matthew's behaviour but as 'Matthew's behaviour being a response to the classteacher's poor organisation and chaotic lessons' that she began to accept that the advice was ill-judged and inappropriate.

The uninvolved professional

In proferring advice from our own perspective we can often reveal our lack of awareness of the parents' lifestyle or culture. On one occasion, an enthusiastic colleague handed out a booklet on 'How to be a super parent' to a family who were struggling to pay the rent. The booklet, full of sound advice, with its middle-class values, the complexity of its language, the family attitudes portrayed and the style of parenting depicted left the family alienated from the worker. The work was delayed by weeks as the support teacher struggled valiantly to re-engage the parents in a cooperative effort for change.

Advice borrowed from elsewhere is rarely appropriate. Far better to work with the people to enable them to develop their next most appropriate strategy. For systemic change to endure, the participants in a given system need to:

- recognise that there is a problem;
- accept that they in some way contribute to its maintenance;
- actively work to do things differently to secure change;
- own the success for the solutions they have found.

The cherished professional

Sometimes the need to be successful and the need to be seen to be successful can get in the way. One of the team working in a primary school setting encountered the situation depicted in Figure 35.

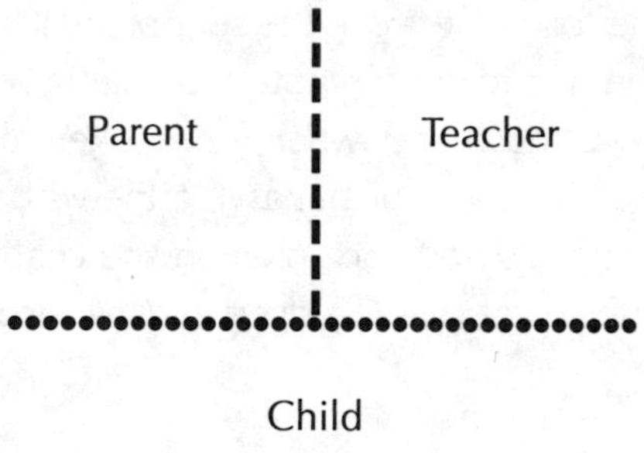

Figure 35

The child, Thomas, a boy aged five, was very attention-seeking and would act out if this attention were not provided immediately. His behaviour could, at times, be extreme, throwing objects and even chairs in class. The support teacher visited both home and school and prepared detailed and specific advice to all the adults as to how they could manage this behaviour. At times the support teacher worked with Thomas, who, bathed in warm supportive adult attention, was angelic for the length of the session.

The support teacher felt the need to run a demonstration of this level of control for the parents. They were suitably impressed. Neither parents nor the classteacher were able to control Thomas' behaviour. As a result no one had been able to effectively implement the advice they had received. In the support teacher's absence things were as bad as ever, both at home and in school.

The parents felt that they had seen the support teacher control the child effectively in the sessions they had witnessed. In their minds Thomas' wellbeing in school became linked with the presence of the support teacher. As all such interventions were time-limited, there came a date when the support teacher withdrew. Without the respite of support, the classteacher felt unable to cope and that Thomas was now much worse. The parents, even though Thomas' behaviour at home was as bad as ever, insisted the school was to blame and that there was an immediate need for the reinstatement of the support. In fact, the parents had lost confidence in their own and the school's competence and declared that they were willing to pay for the support teacher's time. The intervention, instead of contributing to a solution, had now become part of the problem.

In mapping the outcome of this intervention it might look something like Figure 36.

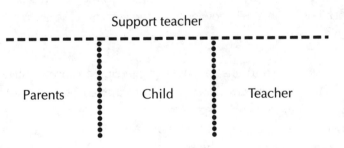

Figure 36

On returning from the closed meeting with the parents the worker concerned was keen to describe to colleagues how important support had become, how needed were the support teachers by both classteachers and the parents. The team who were 'meta' to the system, i.e. detached and objective, spent a great deal of time in helping their colleague to understand that he had made the mistake of:

– owning the problem;
– owning/being the solution;
– disempowering parents and teacher;
– creating long-term dependency.

This needs to be regarded as important or successful as the intervenor becomes very important at the point of closure, a theme that will be revisited later on.

The disappointed/rejected advisor

It is not unusual for pastoral staff and support teachers to feel that they have worked hard with both pupils and parents to effect change only to have their best efforts rejected. Such rejection is difficult to accept and often leaves the worker feeling less kindly disposed towards the pupil and the parents.

In systems terms, what is happening is that the worker is importing in to the system something that simply does not fit. This may be because the advice is not based on a full knowledge of the system. One example will illustrate this.

Having worked hard to enable a pupil to develop a more positive attitude to school and a more effective interaction with the teachers, the support teacher tried to negotiate an effective reward from the parents. She hypothesised that much of the problem behaviour in school had been an attempt to gain attention from the parents.

The pupil concerned had an older sister who had recently become a single parent at sixteen. All the family's attention had focused on the new grandchild and its mother. The support teacher reasoned that, as the girl was now behaving better in school, it was an appropriate time for the parents to reward her with some positive attention. The support teacher suggested that it would be helpful if the parents took their younger daughter clothes shopping in town on the Saturday of the week of the improvement. The suggestion was put to the parents in the presence of their daughter and they agreed to the outing.

In the event it never took place. Mother was babysitting for her older daughter, who herself went out all day on Saturdays. Father was involved in local Saturday sport and on this occasion it was an important cup match. Feeling hurt and rejected, the twelve-year-old ran from the house and did not return home until the early hours of the morning.

In school on Monday, the girl appeared to be very edgy as she told the support teacher of her disappointment and added lurid details about her frightening experiences on the Saturday night. The support teacher shared her anger at the parents with her colleagues. She spoke at length, blaming them for placing their daughter at great risk and for putting her progress in school in jeopardy.

On the face of it this all seems very reasonable, with the teacher justifiably angry with the parents. After all, the suggestion was both achievable and realistic. It seemed such a little thing for parents to do. Furthermore, if they had not intended to do it, why had they not told her so? After much discussion and review of the process of the intervention the support teacher agreed that:

- She had invented the task.
- She had presented it with enthusiasm, ready packaged for the family.
- The parents, seeing her as an important authority figure, accepted her suggestion and offered no opposition to it.
- On the Saturday the demands of their busy lives took over and they failed to deliver the task.
- They were probably feeling doubly guilty and uncomfortable given the events of the Saturday night.

On reflection the support teacher was able to realise that she had generated *an unusable script for the family.* It is always a salutary moment when the worker is made to realise that a script/idea/task which would work in their own home may not be applicable in a different system.

If not advice – then what?

The emphasis has been on working with the process of the subsystems; the way in which people engage with each other, verbally, non-verbally, through a third party and by the unspoken rules by which the subsystem operates.

As has been stated, this means listening to the views of all concerned, their subjective, often discordant views, as well as their detached and more objective statements. This means listening from a participatory but neutral position, tracking what is said, the way in which it is said and at times what is left unsaid. However, when working with more than one person, for example both parents, parents and pupil, or teacher and pupil, there may be a dominant speaker who is presenting all their viewpoint at the expense of the other.

The subordinant participant may be signalling by their non-verbal behaviour – closed body position, turned away, and even shaking heads – that they dispute the view of events being presented. At such a point in time the worker faces a dilemma. If they maintain the neutral position they will only get to hear a part of the story. If they do get the other person's point of view vocalised they may lose the trust and goodwill of the vocal participant. In offering weak support to the non-vocal participant it can often be experienced as patronage – 'I'm sure you must have something to say about this John', or 'Well let's hear what you have to say as you clearly don't agree with what's been said.'

It may be necessary, for a short time, to actively support and even form a brief coalition with this person so that they feel strong enough to fully express their viewpoint in this setting. In getting these things said the worker should try to pick out the positive things being said and mark the negative ones whilst trying not to dwell on *blaming*.

If the support teacher/pastoral team member/psychologist fails to get the subordinate member's views stated, they may only be working with a part of the problem or without the trust of one participant. It is highly unlikely that conflict will get resolved in this way. The potential for a positive outcome is therefore very poor. It is important to remember: when working with more than one individual, silence does not necessary indicate agreement, acceptance or support for a given point of view. Silence can be very angry!

Clarifying and challenging

In listening to people express their view of a problem it is sometimes necessary to clarify what they mean. Members of the support team often found parents and teachers asking questions like 'Are you telling me that this support will really make a difference?' In a sense, the adult is expressing their concern that this may not be a sufficiently weighty intervention to make a difference. At the same time they are passing the onus of the problem back to the worker. There is a great temptation to provide some form of guarantee or assurance based on past success.

What is required is a response that recognises and validates their concern, whilst firmly placing responsibility for the outcome back with them – 'I understand that you are concerned about this. On its own, support is not enough but with *your* help it can be successful.' This kind of message that says – 'This is a very difficult problem do you really have the skills to manage it?' – can come from parents, teachers and even headteachers. The following remark was made by a headteacher in a small primary school: 'We know that David needs clearly defined boundaries and a quick response to the breaking of these boundaries but we feel we've done all we can to control him.'

The worker heard this as saying we really are at the end of our tether with David. At the same time she felt that a second message was being given which was 'Don't blame us for not being firm enough.' At this point she commented on the lengths to which the school had gone in support of David, adding that with support and active involvement from the home, they would certainly succeed.

In a sense, the above is simply clarifying what is being said so that it is clear to all present. At other times it is necessary to make a direct challenge on what is said. To return to Kerry (p. 80), when asked by his father to explain to the worker why he behaved in the way that he did, he offered a litany of excuses: 'I was in with the wrong crowd.' 'The others made me do it.' 'I tried not to but they forced me.'

Kerry could lay blame left and right of him but never at his own door. The author consistently challenged this, pleasantly, politely but firmly. Eventually when explaining why he was late home so often (a major issue with his father and a point for friction that often spilled into school the next day) he said, 'It's true I am late, but sometimes I just don't realise the time.' At this point the author burst out laughing, connected up all Kerry's past excuses with this one and then added, 'I don't think that's how *we* do it; sometimes its so good out where we are that we just decide to stay and risk the row.'

Kerry's response was to smile and agree! In challenging the excuse the worker did so with warmth, *joined* with him, (note the use of *we*), and helped move the issue on from Kerry's initial denial to the real problem. This movement on from the repetitious, excusing phase into the 'real' issues is very helpful in beginning change. Personally, the author has found it useful to challenge most incidents of forgetfulness . . . 'I forgot when it happened.' 'I forgot what I did.' 'I forgot what I saw.' . . . preferring to describe such forgetting as when *we choose not to remember*.

It may be necessary to challenge any member of a subsystem. In working with Kerry and his parents (mother having come out of hospital) the 'problem' changed. Initially when mother came home, she rang to say everything was all right, Kerry was improved at school and at home, and that there was no need for further help. However, the problem had clearly been more longstanding than mother's short admission to hospital and, within three weeks, both school and the family asked for further support.

At the next session the parents offered a different problem. Father described how, when Kerry came in late, he gave him a row and decreed that he would not be going out again for a month! He said that, within days, his wife would give permission to Kerry to go out again. This led to still bigger rows! Father then went on to say that Kerry was an expert at splitting them. He cited instances where Kerry would approach him saying 'Mum says I can go out, but I have to check with you.' In order not to disagree, father acquiesced and agreed to let Kerry go. Later he would discover that Kerry had either not spoken to his mother or only after he had asked his father.

Throughout this, he had been very angry, and concluded with three rapid fire questions: 'Who's to blame? Who really let it happen? Who *is* in charge?' The worker asked Mr Jones to say what he really felt when Kerry made such an approach to go out. Did he really believe that his wife had given permission? Somewhat embarrassed Mr Jones replied, 'Only sometimes.'

The challenge on the problem was then made with the statement, 'Sometimes its hard to be grown up and in charge.' Clearly the problem belonged to the whole parent—child subsystem and it would have been quite unreal to treat it as if it was solely due to Kerry's bad attitude! In systems terms mother and father were not communicating with each other very well. They were content to re-route their communication through Kerry and were risking developing a conflict that detoured through him (see Figures 37 and 38).

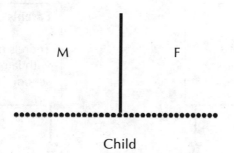

Child

Figure 37

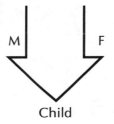

Child

Figure 38

Positive connotation: an acceptable challenge

In trying to secure change, the worker is often attempting to shift the perceptions of the members of the subsystems. Even when an identified individual does manage to change his/her behaviour, unless this is supported by the changed behaviour of those around him/her, the change will not endure and the initial perceptions will still *obtain* (see Figure 39).

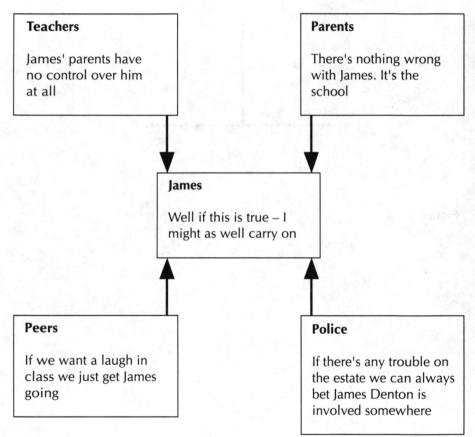

Teachers

James' parents have no control over him at all

Parents

There's nothing wrong with James. It's the school

James

Well if this is true – I might as well carry on

Peers

If we want a laugh in class we just get James going

Police

If there's any trouble on the estate we can always bet James Denton is involved somewhere

Figure 39

Unless the maintaining perceptions of those around him can be shifted, even if the individual wants to change, he finds himself maintained in his role by the expectations of the others. This means that to effect change the worker needs to help the individual change the perceptions of him/herself and also challenge and shift the perceptions of those around him/her. One very benign and effective way in which this can be done is through the use of *positive connotation*. In effect this means listening to the problems, complaints or symptoms described by those making a referral, and then trying to discover a positive aspect in them and then re-presenting this back to the sayer.

Listener	**Speaker**
Screens and positively connotes	Problems, behaviour complaints, difficulties
	Opportunities for change

The reader may recall Kerry's father's behaviour when they left the first support session (p. 81). During a subsequent session Mr Jones was describing the rows they had when Kerry came in late. Again he got as far as saying that, if it continued, Kerry's place in the home was in jeopardy. At this point the worker was able to point out, 'You clearly care a great deal about your son. You go to great lengths to show him how anxious you are about his safety. You even make sure that he doesn't forget his leather jacket.'

It was possible to extend the idea of caring to Kerry's lateness – 'And you, Kerry, keep making sure that dad shows he cares by being so late.' The novelty of this explanation of the redundant cycle of anger that they were caught up in hooked the interest of both of them. In *positively connoting* what had, for both of them, been the unacceptable behaviour of the other, their perceptions were under clear challenge. From then onwards it became increasingly possible to mark all sorts of negative behaviour or problems in a positive light, each time with the suggestion that perhaps there was a better/ more direct way of saying what they felt.

The use of positive connotation cannot be over-stated. Where a system is caught up in a cycle of conflict, with no resolution, a great deal of effort and energy is being wasted in maintaining these positions. This stems from the rigidity of the participants who have been unable to adapt or accommodate to changing circumstances.

In working with difficulties which have a considerable history, there is a need to recognise that people are struggling for things to be better but from too rigid a position. What enables them to give up their position is when they are offered the opportunity to develop a different perception of the problem.

The following examples provide instances where perceptions have been challenged through positive connotation.

At school

– Teacher reports that David is:
  'Very demanding of his parents'.

+ David really wants the time and attention of his parents.

– The classteacher says:
  'I've tried all the strategies that the psychologist recommended without success'.

+ Clearly the classteacher is a committed, flexible professional willing to try new ideas.

– 'She hasn't done anything really nasty yet, like she did last term.'

+ 'Clearly she is now behaving very much better for you.'

The shift to a positive statement helps, not only the person to whom the positive statement is made, but also enables the worker to continue to work positively.

At home

One mother, describing her seven-year-old daughter, Susan:

– 'I can't move for her, she's following me right around the house.'

+ 'Clearly Susan wants your attention, perhaps she needs guaranteed times when she has you to herself?'

A stepfather describing his tantrumming stepson:

– 'He's constantly up to no good. What he needs is a good hard smack every time he misbehaves.'

+ 'You are obviously concerned about his behaviour and want help to find a good way to manage him.'

A mother who was looking very tired and drawn, speaking about the eldest of three boys aged six, four and eighteen months.

—   'I'm beginning to feel that Timothy is getting beyond my control.'

+   'You've managed well so far, but are now seeking a different way of doing things.'

This approach becomes even more effective when two subsystems are in conflict with each other. The following extracts are statements drawn from a real example.

1. **Headteacher**   I feel that father is actively encouraging Carol to behave badly in school.

2. **Classteacher**   When I try to reprimand Carol she responds by shouting that she will tell mum and dad.

3. **Parents**   The headteacher is always picking on Carol. She gets punished more than any other kid in school.

4. **Parents**   It's the classteacher's fault, if she had more control of the class Carol wouldn't start her nonsense.

Clearly, in this example drawn from an intervention in the first junior year of a primary school, matters have almost reached impasse. Relationships between home and school have deteriorated to the point where communication is by Carol or a third party (Figure 40).

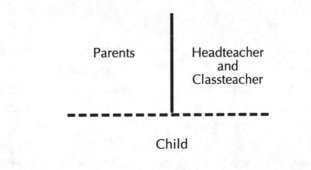

Parents   Headteacher
               and
               Classteacher

Child

Figure 40

Positive connotation in such an extreme case, though difficult, is necessary in enhancing the chances of a successful outcome. Readers might like to consider how they could positively connote the statements made by the headteacher, classteacher and parents. The following are the responses that the team conjured with.

1. **To headteacher**   You seem to be saying that if we can get father to work with us, Carol will improve.

   To father   The headteacher feels that you can exert a great deal of effective control over Carol.

2. **To classteacher**   Carol clearly sees mum and dad as powerful people, we need them to work with us to control her in school.

   To parents   Carol sees you as being very powerful. She even threatens people that she will tell you about them. She needs to know that you support the other adults who care about her.

3. **To parents**   It seems that the headteacher is prepared to spend a lot of time and effort to help Carol.

4. **To parents**   You seem to be saying you would like to see more control, not less, in school. Would you consider working with the school to help control Carol?

Clearly this is a very condensed version of a lengthy piece of work, but it does help to highlight that what is stated as a complaint or a difficulty can often be restated as a positive that will help change perceptions. It is not a universal panacea and at times it can be difficult to generate positives, particularly when working in isolation or when the situation seems to be deteriorating.

As a team it proved helpful to discuss individual problems, particularly those that seemed most negative, to see if the group could restate elements of the problem in positive terms. Even then, the positive connotation has to fit both the person who says it and the situation in which they use it, or it will not be usable, as in the example below.

On one occasion, in a discussion, a support teacher expressed her anger at the recent exclusion of a pupil she had been working with. She explained how she had worked hard with the team of teachers who taught Malcolm (aged fourteen) and with his parents and felt she had enabled everyone to adopt positions which could effect change. Matters were beginning to work well and everyone had noticed his improved attitude and behaviour in class. Then a dinner lady (not seen as part of an important subsystem in the initial referral) had challenged Malcolm's place in a queue and had tried to lead him to the back of it. He told her to '———— off.' She complained to the headteacher who, given Malcolm's past record, saw it as being *more of the same* and excluded him for ten days, without consulting with any of the pastoral staff involved with Malcolm.

After much discussion and debate about the waste of a costly intervention and the lack of consultation and communication in the school, the worker was asked to state what she wanted to happen next. Her key aim was to have the headteacher behave in a more consultative way. The team suggested that the worker:

- Positively connote the headteacher's prompt action.
- Positively connote his making Malcolm safe.
- Positively connote his support for pupils and staff in school.
- Suggest that prompt exclusion from school and prompt return might enable Malcolm to sustain progress, thus making school easier for staff and pupils alike.

As a group we were very pleased that we had successfully struggled to find positives in such a negative situation. However, all to no avail, when the support teacher concerned tried to turn these ideas into things to say to the headteacher she found that they felt and sounded false and did not really fit the situation.

For readers who are interested in the use of positive connotation Molnar and Lindquist (1989) provide many examples of such usage in an American context. (Cautionary note: some of the examples are clearly culturally grounded and to a British ear would sound glib or naive.)

The following examples provide the opportunity to try to positively connote things said by parents, pupils and teachers. Try them yourself.

- Janice never manages to finish any of her classwork.
+

- Gareth truanted on both Tuesday and Thursday afternoon.
+

- Susan's mother keeps coming in to school to tell us how to teach her daughter.
+

—   Mr Evans always checks that I've done my homework, as if I am the only one!

+

—   Colin Watkins has started to behave just like his brother used to.

+

Some sample answers can be found in Appendix 3 on page 125.

One classic example of a positive connotation made to a pupil by a support teacher came when a thirteen-year-old pupil complained that he felt conspicuous and uncomfortable having a support teacher to help him. The support teacher offered the response, 'You seem to be saying that you would like to try to manage on your own in school. That's excellent. If you find that you cannot manage and start misbehaving again, then I will assume that you are asking for my help once more.'

On first hearing it may seem like a verbal conundrum but she cleverly restated his objection as a wish to manage his own behaviour, then adding that future misbehaviour would not be seen as him being 'bad' but as him asking for help. His behaviour improved dramatically as a consequence.

Finding the solution

In working with subsystems, the support team often used the technology of behaviour modification and the interpersonal skills and insight of the psychodynamic approach. However, these were always applied through the framework of a systems methodology. In essence, this means ensuring that all those involved in the problem become involved in determining the solution. Inadvertently this was the approach being used in the intervention with Amanda (pp. 16–24).

In practice, this can happen very quickly and bring immediate results but, in other instances, time is needed to win people's trust in the process before they commit themselves to finding a solution. A ready example of the way in which a solution can be quickly found is evident in the case of Kerry (pp. 80–1, 93–5). A big issue in the family appeared to be Kerry's lateness home. Having positively connoted the behaviour of father and son they were able to begin to break free of their redundant cycle of activity (see Figure 41).

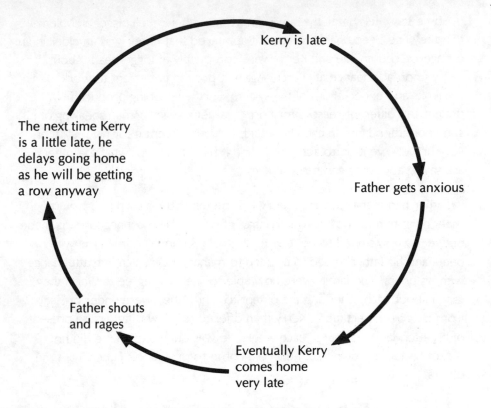

Kerry is late

Father gets anxious

Eventually Kerry comes home very late

Father shouts and rages

The next time Kerry is a little late, he delays going home as he will be getting a row anyway

Figure 41

Once they both accepted this different reality it was possible to ask them what should be done about it. The solution was readily provided by Kerry who simply said, 'They should keep me in for two nights when I'm late.' On the face of it this sounded both realistic and fair. Father, asked for his solution suggested an even more reasonable approach, 'When Kerry may be late he has to ring home, saying where he is and how long he will be.'

These may seem to be obvious ideas to people not expending huge amounts of energy in a redundant cycle. Kerry and his father had no time or energy to search for such a solution. What is more, neither would initially have heard the other's suggestion. This acceptance and accommodation to each other would not have been possible whilst they both held to their blaming positions. Having begun to negotiate appropriate limits and boundaries, the family rapidly agreed ways of managing lateness, truancy, successful work performance in school etc. In a very short time they were able to establish a new and effective way of transacting together. At this point, support was withdrawn and both the family and the school were congratulated on *their* successful resolution of *their* difficulties.

Some six weeks later the family returned with a 'much bigger' problem that they had been unable to solve. It appeared that father was an elder in an evangelical church. He and Kerry were completely at loggerheads about Kerry's non-attendance at church. Again, it proved important to work within the limits and expectations of the system. Further probing produced two distinct and different reasons for Kerry's father's anger. When speaking of his son's non-attendance in church he said, 'I cannot accept it for his soul', then very bravely went on to add, 'And I find it hard to accept what the others are saying about my son not attending.'

Father had managed to tell Kerry that he felt that his own peers were sneering at him for not being in control of his son. The connection was made between Kerry's need to be seen to control his coming home time with his peers and his father's need to be seen to manage Kerry's church attendance with his peers. The family were now able to see the degree to which they cared about each other and the extent to which they were under pressure from outside expectations. Kerry then offered to give his father the present of his attendance at church each week. He was quite explicit, he did not accept his father's belief but he would come to protect his father from the others.

One might argue that this is not a perfect solution but it was *their* solution and therefore much more likely to be attempted with commitment and to endure. At this point it was possible to restate the position of Kerry at home and in school and to *positively reframe* both systems.

The team learned to help families, pupils and teachers refine the ways in which they addressed their difficulties. Not to impose, not to prescribe but to enable. In many cases there were parents, teachers and pupils who had given up trying to make things work and viewed any further efforts as pointless. They often stated the problem as being without hope early in the first meeting. Such statements tend to seem like challenges to the interventionist's skills and abilities. There is a perceived need to provide reassurance and to provide either an optimistic view of the future or a guarantee of a successful outcome!

Such responses tend to disqualify the participants' view of their difficulties. There is a danger that we signal that we have the answer and that our presence will in some way secure effective change. Such an optimistic view can appear to be patronising and even rude as the worker is failing to *join* the participants in their experience of the problem. Such a failure can further disempower parents and teacher colleagues and in structural terms the worker is placing him/herself in the adult layer above them.

To prevent this happening there is a need to ensure that the worker responds from what is known as the *one-down position*. This means working hard to signal an acceptance that matters are as bad as they are being presented and that there are no ready made quick-fix solutions. The statements below try to illustrate the use of the *one-down position*.

Initial statement	'Expert' response	The one-down response
Parent 1 Well, we've done everything for David but it has got us nowhere.	Well I am sure there are some things still to be tried.	I can't imagine how hard you have had to work with him.
Parent 2 I washed my hands of her long ago.	We all feel like that sometimes but I'm sure that you really do care.	How did you manage to keep on trying for so long?
Teacher 1 Well there's no point trying a contract – we've had three since I've been teaching Jake.	Contracts are quite technical things, perhaps we can try a different format.	Three contracts? How did you make them seem fresh each time?
Teacher 2 I've never known a seven-year-old as aggressive as Jonathan.	Oh we've changed the behaviour of much more difficult children than John.	I don't know how you have coped with him in such a large class.

The 'expert' responses have some obvious risks attached to them. They can sound sympathetic but there is a clear danger that they may be patronising. Such remarks may not give due recognition that the problems are as great as the first speakers describe them. Equally they may imply that we as newcomers to their system know much more than they do. By contrast the one-down replies are intended to confirm that:

1. This is a serious situation.
2. Change will not be easy.
3. The parents/teachers have been working very hard to cope with the situation.
4. They are the experts i.e. have in-depth knowledge of the problem.

One of the remarkable outcomes from such an approach is that teachers and parents respond by explaining all the ways in which they have tried to manage their difficulties. The level of effort, amount of time and degree of ingenuity they have utilised in trying to solve their problem provides useful insight into what further steps they may be able to sustain in working for change.

The central issue is that the person planning the intervention has not owned or taken over the problem. It remains firmly with the adults within the system.

Minuchin, at the London Conference anticipating the Children's Act in 1989; describes working from the one-down position as the use of *strategic incompetence*. He described this as being a learned skill and is best exemplified when the expert is able to say 'I need your help to understand this.'

Chapter 8

Developing a systems solution to the referral of Edward Morgan

Throughout this text snippets of examples of the work involved in particular interventions have been used to illustrate a particular point. This example explores one case in depth, to describe both the problems and potential of working this way.

The referral

Edward Morgan, aged eight years seven months, was one of three boys referred from the same school. He had always presented problems in school but there had been an ongoing acceptance of his particular difficulties following any incident. Provided Edward was not confronted by an adult, he would eventually calm down and return to class. If challenged he would 'flip', go into a rage, break out of school, run away or shin up the nearest drainpipe or tree.

Preliminary views
School's view
The classteacher   Edward has been a problem since nursery school. It's proved better not to confront his behaviour as he will simply generate an even greater problem. He sits apart in class, doing the work that he chooses and will not join in assemblies or other large groups. He is best controlled by asking him for his help, as he is always ready to lend a hand.

The headteacher The situation is now impossible (following an advisory visit). Edward's behaviour is completely beyond control and unless things change he will have to be moved.

The family view

Mum, pregnant with her third child, said that the school had tried to cope with Edward and had accepted a great deal of bad behaviour from him. 'He is *very* difficult at school but not so bad at home.' She said he behaves badly with his grandfather but wouldn't dare to try it with his grandmother.

The pupil's view

Unknown. When approached in class he hid under a desk and refused to engage with anyone.

Further information

Subsystem 1 – pupil and teacher

Two classroom observations revealed that Edward was socially and spatially isolated in class. He was further separated from others by the 'different' nature of his work.

The classteacher spoke of having tried the whole range of sanctions and rewards including 'involving Edward's mother!' Even so, Mrs Galpin the classteacher exonerated Edward, saying 'No wonder he behaves as he does, given the home he is from.'

Mrs Galpin was angry as she spoke about Edward's position but both warm and maternal when speaking of Edward himself. At the end of the session she concluded 'We've tried everything and are ready to give up with him now.'

Subsystem 2 – parent and pupil

The support teacher met with mum and son in school and then at home. (The initial meeting was at school as she regularly collected Edward.) She spoke warmly about her son, agreeing with what the school had said about him. She described his difficulties with almost a degree of pride in terms of the level of problems he presented. She explained she was pregnant for a third time by the same man, although stressing that he did not live with them, but just stayed for a few nights each week. She explained that Edward always ran away from a telling off and that the only person to control him was her mother, Edward's grandmother. Overall she presented as feeling helpless and a victim of Edward's difficult behaviour.

Mapping the system

The structural map of the system in which Edward was involved seemed to be as shown in Figure 42.

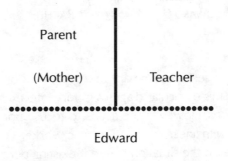

Figure 42

Both his mother and his classteacher seemed to be over-involved and enmeshed in his behaviour. Neither of them presented as being able to challenge him successfully. Despite their common concern they had stopped communicating effectively with each other regarding their joint management of Edward.

A second diagram of Edward's family (Figure 43) may help clarify his background. For those unfamiliar with the conventions of a geneogram see Appendix 1.

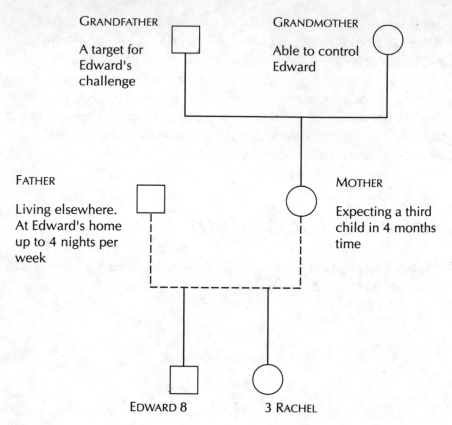

GRANDFATHER

A target for
Edward's
challenge

GRANDMOTHER

Able to control
Edward

FATHER

Living elsewhere.
At Edward's home
up to 4 nights per
week

MOTHER

Expecting a third
child in 4 months
time

EDWARD 8   3 RACHEL

Figure 43

The geneogram is in a sense a summary of a great deal of social and familial information. Clearly this particular diagram is very interesting and prompts many further questions. However, the aim is to focus upon the process and not get sidetracked with linear information. The worker has to try to establish the positives in the situation to see if existing perceptions of Edward can be challenged.

Marking the positives

Subsystem 1 – in school

- — Edward sat in class at a seat on his own.
- + Mrs Galpin could isolate Edward in class if necessary.

- — Edward 'worked' at classroom tasks that he chose.
- + Edward was anxious to appear to work like other children.

- — Mrs Galpin had used the whole range of rewards and sanctions to try to manage Edward.
- + Mrs Galpin was flexible enough to look at a range of management methods.

- — Mrs Galpin felt that Edward's home was a causative factor.
- + Mrs Galpin recognised that home required help to manage Edward effectively.

- — Mrs Galpin was maternal and protective of Edward to the point of over-involvement.
- + Mrs Galpin liked him.

Subsystem 2 – at home

Marking areas of possible change.

- — Mum was pregnant again with her third child.
- + Mum has a stable relationship with a man who is father of all three children.

- — Mum was amused by Edward's misdemeanours.
- + Mum could recognise his misbehaviour but did not yet know how best to respond to it.

- — Mum felt helpless in the face of Edward's rage.
- + Mum had a good role model in her own mother as to how to manage Edward's rage behaviour.

- — Mum was said to be apathetic and said as much about herself in an interview.
- + Mum attended both initial meetings.

These ideas were then discussed with the members of the team who helped the worker develop a way of approaching the problem from a systems position.

The ideas are connected and linked to try to *reframe* the problem, that is to present it in a new and different way. It is important that both subsystems have the opportunity to change their perceptions at or around the same time to maximise the forces for change. Presenting a reframed view of a subsystem is a demanding task, it requires the ability to work with warmth, empathy, genuineness and at times firmness with participants.

Reframing 1

Subsystem 1 – in school

Existing perceptions were challenged with Mrs Galpin. It was marked that:

1. Edward was not beyond control as his maternal grandmother could manage him.
2. Mrs Galpin liked Edward and that was obvious, and he liked her.
3. Mrs Galpin could place Edward in the class each lesson at a distance from her that reflected how hard he had tried in the last lesson.
4. In this way she could reduce his isolation and expand his wish to appear to work like the other children in class.
5. Mrs Galpin had shown great flexibility in the past in her attempts to manage Edward and the support teacher was confident that this strategy was relatively straightforward for a teacher with her skills and experience.
6. Home needed to be guided in its support of Edward and so she, Mrs Galpin, could use a reporting system to help 'shape' Mum's responses.
7. If matters deteriorated, the maternal grandmother would also be involved as a support for control in the home.

Mrs Galpin had little difficulty in accepting points 1–5. She readily agreed that the grandmother would certainly be a positive force for good – as she had been in the past. Mrs Galpin was less convinced that Edward's mother had the ability to change. This reluctant to take a positive view of mum stemmed from Mrs Galpin's recollections of how difficult Edward's mother had been in school. After further discussion she declared herself prepared to try.

It is important to note that in only getting Mrs Galpin to accept part of the reframe – we the intervention team still had some work to do. It proved to be much easier to offer a new way of looking at the system to Edward's mother, the key ideas being:

Subsystem 2 – at home

Existing perceptions were challenged with mum by:

1. Noting her attendance at meetings and her concern for Edward.

2. Highlighting her amusement at some of Edward's antics and asking her to find a new way of responding.
3. Marking that she might seek these new ways by using the role model of her own mother.
4. Indicating that as both Mrs Galpin and she cared about Edward they needed to work together in harmony to prevent Edward becoming confused.

Experiencing the new subsystems

Meetings were held at intervals with Mrs Galpin the classteacher, Edward's mother and Edward to try to secure a new way of interacting. This interaction was focused upon the ways in which the adults in each subsystem reported and responded to Edward's changed behaviour.

The intervention met with some initial success. There was an immediate small short-term gain in Edward's behaviour. After a few weeks there seemed to be a relapse and matters were as bad as ever. Mrs Galpin announced that she was simply not up to the task in class and that Edward had to go. Edward's mother accepted this view and agreed that all that was possible had now been done.

The support teacher felt at a loss as to how to proceed, particularly now that things had deteriorated after initial success. The colleague invited in to help, offered the view that Edward was not a severely disturbed little boy beyond his own control. The opinion was expressed that Edward knew what he was doing and was not convinced that the adults around him really intended to take control. Further interviews revealed that the intervention had inadvertently reinforced one of the maintaining factors in the problem.

The involvement of Edward's grandmother had had an unforeseen effect. Grandmother's involvement in the direct parenting of Edward displaced mother in her attempts to take control of him. The effect of grandmother's better, firmer control was to place Edward's mother in the subordinate or child position and so diminished her own ability to parent her son. This interaction was made worse when grandmother collected Edward from school. Maternal grandmother and classteacher shared a mutual concern for Edward. They both accepted each other as competent adults but both felt Edward's mother was unable to cope. In effect they treated mother as much as a child as Edward (Figure 43). This new view of the system was shared with Edward's mother who agreed that at times that was how it felt.

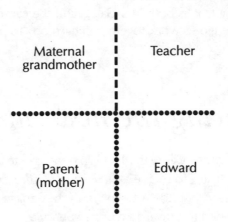

Maternal grandmother | Teacher

Parent (mother) | Edward

Figure 44

Edward's mother then introduced further information about the family. She explained that Edward's father, a labourer, was virtually living at home full time. Despite this domestic arrangement, maternal grandmother refused to have anything to do with him. This new information that we had been engaged with only a part of the subsystem led to the offer of an appointment to meet with mother, father and Edward. Initially this was said to be impossible as father worked until at least 5.30 pm each night. An appointment was offered at 6.30 pm and held in school.

The meeting began slowly, but it emerged that at the present time:

1. Father was banned from managing Edward's behaviour.
2. For two nights each week Edward stayed with his grandmother.

Edward's behaviour was then positively connoted as being intended to force his father to take charge of him, both privately at home and publicly in school. This would demonstrate to everyone that father was committed to the family and that he cared about Edward. Father's significance in generating a positive outcome was strongly marked.

Father was keen to try to help. The parents were then asked to work together to agree ways in which they could reward Edward's good behaviour in school. The only guidance offered was that the rewards were not to be financial or material, as the family's resources were limited. The rewards they were asked to devise should involve Edward having the chance to spend time in the company of one or both parents.

At the next meeting the parents reported that if Edward sustained a good week in school then father might take him: dog racing at the local track, fishing in the local river, or football training at the local club. (Note – these may not be ideal or perfect activities but they fitted well within the family's culture and were therefore more likely to be implemented.)

This progress was reported back to school only to be met with the response, 'They're both very plausible, but they'll never sustain anything. We know him (father) of old.' (It later emerged that staff in school suspected Edward's father in participating in a recent burglary of the school!)

At the next session with the parents they were asked to decide what sanction they might use for responding to Edward's difficult behaviour in school. The only guidance offered was they might think in terms of what Edward might least like to lose. Somewhat tentatively they agreed to curb Edward's visits to his grandmother's if he misbehaved in school. Later it emerged that Edward's nights at his grandmother's were the parents' nights out with the darts team.

In school Mrs Galpin was asked to return to her old way of functioning, that is not to sanction Edward, simply to return a fair and accurate reportage of his behaviour to Edward's parents. The classteacher's scepticism was confronted with the response that as these were the only parents Edward had we should really try to support their efforts to be 'good enough' parents.

During the following fortnight the support teacher twice confronted Edward about his behaviour and he raged his way through his refusal to accede to adult request. (It was felt that these rages still demonstrated Edward's doubts in the certainty of the adults' commitment to help.) Throughout this time his parents responded as promised and used the agreed sanctions.

Three weeks later Edward was reported as being much changed, he had:
– had no negative comments from his classteacher;
– been dog racing with his father;

- been fishing with his father;
- brought a song book to school;
- brought in a picture of his mother's class when she had been a pupil in the school.

From this point forward the system had changed. Edward had discovered that he could behave – that he could be accepted by other pupils and that both his parents cared enough to take control of him. This does not mean that Edward, the referred problem was cured, rather the system had become unstuck and was changing. It would be for the participants to determine the direction of this change.

Giving away success

Mrs Galpin was delighted at the changes in Edward. She tried hard to insist that all the positive change was due to the work of the support teacher in two school-based confrontations of Edward's rage. She found it very hard to accept that the support teacher gave all credit to both the parents and Mrs Galpin for their efforts. (There is a great temptation to accept the praise and own the success of such a complex intervention. Yet in systems thinking there is a need to reinforce the participants' sense of their own success so that they can confidently rely on each other in the future.)

Edward's parents expressed their joy in the changes wrought in his behaviour both at home and in school. They were extremely grateful to the teacher for her patience and forbearance with Edward both in the recent and more distant past. They needed to be strongly encouraged to see and own their key part in Edward's success. As for Edward, he managed to say how pleased he was with school and home and how other children seemed to like him now.

Remapping the system

The support teacher had been a very successful agent of change. She had brought together all the components of the system around the referred pupil and harnessed all the available energy for change. This had involved a sustained rebuilding of the structures of the system.

The initial difficulties were symptomatic of our limited view of the parental subsystem. In structural terms the system can be remapped – see Figure 45. In the longer term the unforgiving nature of the relationship between maternal grandmother and Edward's father suggests that all is not well. It may be that if the family system fails to continue to adapt then the same or new problems will emerge.

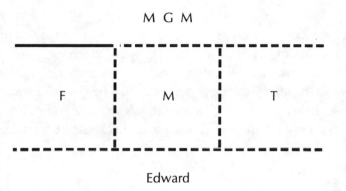

Figure 45

The importance of never owning the problem and never owning the solution was clearly and amusingly reinforced when one of the support team worked with an eight-year-old boy called Philip. Philip was referred for a multiplicity of difficulties. Philip's classteacher, parents and grandparents all agreed to work together to secure a positive outcome. In the review meeting some eight weeks later everybody reported on Philip's changed behaviour – he didn't steal, swear or quarrel anymore. At home his mother reported that Philip now did as he was asked, ran errands for her, laid the table and made his own bed in the morning. It was at this point that Philip's grandfather intervened to complain, 'He's over-cured. He's too good. You've taken the boy out of him. He's become a cardboard copy of his old self.'

Chapter 9

Getting to work systemically

This book describes the work of a team of teachers who struggled to develop a systems approach to problem behaviour in schools. As is evident, the team did not always experience success or gain ready insight into the methodology. Together we struggled to provide a new and fresh impetus to the difficulties being experienced by the schools within one LEA. In reflecting upon that experience there seem to be some critical lessons for securing success:

Working systemically at the macro level

There is a need to secure support for the methodology at the macro level. In this instance, as the organisation was the LEA, there was a need to secure support for the model at the political level – through member involvement; at the senior officer level – i.e. within the directors' team; and at the school level – through the engagement of headteachers and teacher representatives.

The involvement of these three groups in the design of the approach ensured that there was sustained ownership and support for the style of intervention. The same would be true at the school level. There is a need to secure key stakeholder support for this type of work in the form of governors, headteachers and teacher representatives. Without such support the workers, whatever their roles risk being disqualified by those they are trying to support. It is essential that everyone is made aware that the methodology being used is new and different.

Establish clear boundaries

The Dealing with Difficulty team worked in schools on the basis of up to four sessions, each of one hour, each week, for up to eight weeks. The use of a definite time boundary helped in focusing the thoughts of all concerned, who realised that they had extra help, but of limited duration. In effect this ensured engagement and focused effort right from the start of the intervention.

If the intervention is open-ended then there is a risk that the intervention drifts and that the person providing the support finds themselves owning the problem. The use of the time boundary both over the length of the intervention and with regard to each individual session enhances people's use of limited support time and ensures that the support resource is constantly released to be used elsewhere.

The use of clear boundaries is much more difficult when trying to work from a within-school position, such as a member of the pastoral team. Colleagues often value the ready availability and flexibility of the pastoral staff. Nevertheless in indicating to colleagues, parents and pupils the amount of time available to address a particular problem the pastoral teacher is helping them to measure their effective use of his/her time. Effective boundaries include functional boundaries – Is the problem a legitimate referral for the attention of the pastoral staff? The exercise on page 71 helps to clarify this matter.

Determine clear roles

Whether it be from within or outside the school it needs to be clearly established that the intervention is to enable those experiencing the problem to make progress. It is *not* to manage the problem on their behalf. In every sense it needs to be made evident that the support on offer is conditional upon those being supported making every effort to use such help well. Colleagues who signal that they, in making the referral, are washing their hands of the problem are simply reducing the effectiveness of any intervention and at the same time using up too much of what is a finitely limited resource.

In establishing clear roles, it is important to remember that many colleagues attempt to distance themselves from the problem and hand it over to someone else. This is not simply their rejection of an individual, rather it is often due to the challenge and threat the problem poses to their professional skills. The address on this problem is complex and needs to include the provision of school-based training for all staff.

Working at the referral level

In the experience of the author, it is very difficult to work from a systems position as an individual. Even within the context of a close, supportive, like-minded team it is all too easy to slip into linear thinking or to focus upon interesting aspects of a problem instead of the process and working towards a solution.

In making the shift to a systems methodology there is a need to work with at least one other like-minded colleague with whom one can transact in the language and concepts of systems thinking. As a team of ten people working in a common role and meeting weekly to discuss problems and review progress there were times when as a group we collectively lost the objective position and started owning the problem or blaming others for our lack of success.

Work from the 'meta' or objective position

This means that instead of making your first subjective response to the situation, stand back and try to see the process that is maintaining the problem. Then work with the subsystems that sustain this process. In this way you can plan your critical point of entry to the system. By working to make the best use of yourself as a scarce resource try to harness all the potential forces for change around the referred problem. This will mean using the skills of systems engagement to join with the subsystems, connote the positives, challenge the existing perceptions and then reframe the problem so that others can see it in a new light. This approach should ensure that you work to best effect, generating maximal impact through optimum input.

If you succeed in beginning the process of change, *never own the problem nor the solution* as together they represent an ongoing burden that is too great. If you do slip into this position then it is very difficult to negotiate an effective withdrawal.

The ideas outlined in this book have helped in the delivery of an effective response to a wide variety of entrenched problematic situations. By working from a systems position it has been possible to draw upon a range of psychological concepts and integrate them into an effective approach to very stuck situations. Systems thinking allows the worker – whether father, head of year, psychologist or social worker – to harness all the people involved in the referred problem in a sustained attempt to effect change. It takes time to absorb these ideas and to use them with proficiency. They are much more readily acquired through an apprenticeship model, within a team sharing this form of thinking. For the enthusiastic committed professional there is the possibility of acquiring these concepts through in-depth further reading.

The appreciation of the time worth of systems thinking comes at the moment of reawakening, when the individual, the teacher and the family realise that *they* can change matters and that *they* will do so. In that heady moment, when the members of the system take charge of it and redefine their interaction together, it takes great self-discipline to applaud their achievement rather than claim one's own success.

Appendix 1

Geneogram

This is a diagrammatic way of describing the structure of a family. The format used in this book is as follows:

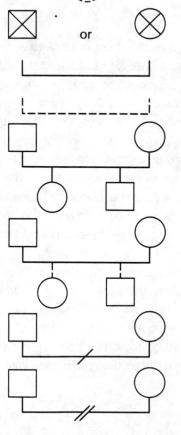

Living male family member

Living female family member

Unborn child

Deceased family members

or

Marriage

Non-formalised relationship

Blood relationships between
parents and children

Non-blood relationship
between parents and children

Separation

Divorce

This convention allows the professional to see quite complex family structures at a glance.

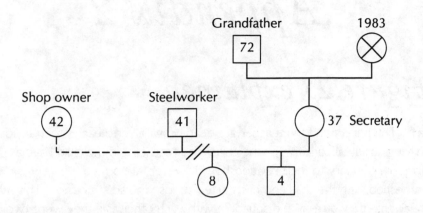

Appendix 2

Figure 25 explained

(**a**)   The parent and the teacher are readily available to each other as adults sharing a mutual concern for the child. The teacher and the child have a proper boundary to their relationship. However, at home the parent is enmeshed with the child and has started to lose the adult position. This may mean that they quarrel and squabble with each other as if they were two children together. This can become problematic in school when either:

- the child tries to treat his/her teacher in the same way as he/she treats the parent; or
- the parent comes into school, perhaps to fight the child's battle with another pupil.

(**b**)   Shows the teacher and the parent appropriately engaged as are the teacher and the pupil. The parent is however quite detached from the child. This may take the form of a physical inaccessibility, such as working unsocial hours, or an emotional inaccessibility, for example the parent is depressed and self-absorbed. If the child needs parental support to meet a crisis it may not be readily available to him/her.

(**c**)   In this example it is the teacher who is too detached and remote, perhaps conveying the attitude of, 'I am simply here to teach my subject – I am not concerned with the wider welfare of children.' This would become problematic if the child required adult support to deal with a problem such as being bullied.

(**d**)   This is the converse of (**a**) where the teacher has become enmeshed with the child and has started to lose the adult position. This might take the form of over-concern with the performance and progress of one child as compared to the rest of the class – perhaps the teacher's pet syndrome?

These are all fairly low-key problems that cause only minor concern to those involved.

Appendix 3

Positive connotation

+   With more time Janice could probably finish her classwork.

+   Gareth managed four days full attendance this week.

+   Susan's mother is very motivated when it comes to her daughter's reading.

+   Mr Evans clearly thinks you're a pupil worth bothering about.

+   As you've taught his brother you'll know the mistakes to avoid.

Bibliography

BANDURA, A. (1983) *Aggression – A Social Learning Analysis.* London: Prentice Hall.

BATESON, G. (1972) *Steps to an Ecology of Mind.* New York: Chandler.

BULL, S. L. and SOLLITY, J. (1987) *Classroom Management – Principles to Practice.* London: Croom Helm.

BURDEN, R. L. (1978) School Systems Analysis in GILLHAM, B. (ed.) *Reconstructing Educational Psychology.* London: Croom Helm.

DES (1989) *Discipline in School. (The Elton Committee Report.) London: HMSO.*

DOWLING, E. and OSBORNE, E. (1985) The Family and the School. London: Routledge and Kegan Paul.

FRUGGERI, L. (1990) 'Organisational Burn Out' presented at the Systemic Family Therapy Conference, Cardiff.

GORDON, T. (1970) *Parent Effectiveness Training.* New York: Wyden.

HAMBLIN, D. (1984) *Pastoral Care – A Training Manual.* Oxford: Basil Blackwell.

HERBERT, M. (1975) *Conduct Disorders of Childhood and Adolescence.* Chichester: Wiley.

HERBERT, M. (1988) *Working with Children and their Families.* B.P.S. London: Routledge and Kegan Paul.

MIECHENBAUM, D. (1972) *Cognitive Behaviour Modification.* New York: Plennm.

MINUCHIN, S. (1974) *Families and Family Therapy.* London: Tavistock Publications.

MINUCHIN, S. and FISHMANN, H. C. (1981) *Family Therapy Techniques.* Cambridge, Mass: Harvard University Press.

MINUCHIN, S. (1984) *The Family Kaleidoscope.* Cambridge, Mass: Harvard University Press.

MOLNAR, A. and LINDQUIST, B. (1989) *Changing Problem Behaviour in Schools.* San Francisco: Jossey Bass.

MONGON, D. and HART, S. with ACE, C. and RAWLINGS, A. (1989) *Improving Classroom Behaviour: New Directions for Teachers and Pupils.* London: Cassell.

NOVACO, K. (1975) *Anger Control.* Lexington: Lexington Press.

O'DONNEL, C. R. and WORRELL, L. (1973) Motor and cognitive relaxation in the desensitisation of anger. *Behaviour Research and Therapy,* Vol. 11, 473–81.

PALAZZOLI, M. S. (1989) *Family Games.* London: Karnac.

RIMM, D. C. et al. (1971) Systemic desensitisation of an anger response. *Behaviour Research and Therapy,* Vol. 9, 273–80.

ROBERTSON, J. (1989) *Effective Classroom Control.* Sevenoaks: Hodder and Stoughton.

ROSE, M. (1990) *Healing Hurt Minds.* London: Tavistock Routledge.

SHUTTLEWORTH, R. (1983) Wheels Within Wheels: A Systems Approach to Maladjustment. *Maladjustment and Therapeutic Education* 1.2: 32–40.

SKINNER, B. F. (1953) *Science and Human Behaviour.* New York: Macmillan.

SKYNNER, R. and CLEESE, J (1983) *Families and How to Survive Them.* London: Miranda.

SPEED, B. (1984) Family Therapy: An Update. Newsletter of Association of Child Psychology and Psychiatry 6.1. 2–14.

UPTON, G. and COOPER, P. (1990) A New Perspective on Behaviour Problems in Schools: The Ecosystemic Approach. *Maladjustment and Therapeutic Education,* Vol. 8, No. 1.

VON BERTALANFFY, L. (1950) The Theory of Open Systems in Physics and Biology. *Science,* 3, 25–9.

WHELDALL, K. and MERRIT, F. (1984) *Positive Teaching – The Behavioural Approach.* London: Unwin Educational.